I0211667

Resurrecting Worship

"Worship is our response to all that God is, says, and does. Even though the generations may respond differently, it is not how we worship but whom we worship. Joseph Lear has a deep conviction to see the practice of biblical worship be a catalyst for spiritual growth."

—**DOUG CLAY**, general superintendent, Assemblies of God

"I am glad that Joseph has written this book and that he is publishing it now. We need it, more than ever."

—**CHRIS GREEN**, professor, public theology, Southeastern University, Lakeland, Florida, from the foreword

"In *Resurrecting Worship*, Joseph Lear takes us on a journey of theological depth and worship innovation that blends the best of Protestant liturgy and Pentecostal tradition. It is the hands-on story of the transformation of a smaller, lower-income, multicultural church into an authentic community of Christ's followers who serve and love. Read it with an open mind and a hungry heart!"

—**JAMES BRADFORD**, lead pastor, Central Assembly of God

"The dynamic combination of Pentecost and liturgy are on display in *Resurrecting Worship*. Joseph Lear uses engaging stories and testimonies from a middle-America church to display how we can love God and neighbors with equal passion. If you are ready to see your church and community through a fresh perspective, I invite you to join me in being impacted by this book."

—**DAVID DOCUSEN**, author of *Neighborliness: Love Like Jesus. Cross Dividing Lines. Transform Your Community.*

"Joseph's commitment to scholarship and Pentecostal worship redefined is clear in his writing. Drawing from his work in Iowa, he masterfully weaves in the experiences there and offers considerations for the broader church. In our tradition, there is a broad spectrum of expressions, and he unpacks thoughtful insights that are sincere and reveal his dedication to leading an authentic Spirit-filled community at the grass roots. His treatment of Pentecostal worship is both insightful and gracious. By emphasizing the centrality of Scripture, the significance of prophetic preaching, and the role of communal worship, he offers a perspective on worship that will deepen the readers knowledge of ecclesiology—all intended to strengthen the local church."

—**MIKE RAKES**, president, Evangel University

"For a world—and a church—addicted to the fast and furious, Joseph Lear reimagines the gathered people of God. Lear interrogates elaborate worship schemes that strive primarily for relevance and effectiveness. He envisions, instead, a church that creates a trinitarian, eucharistic, and Pentecostal liturgy. Lear does not offer yet another 'how-to' manual, but he offers a path toward prayer-filled, embodied, and celebratory liturgy. I recommend this book for every Assemblies of God pastor on a quest for a slow burn revival."

—**MARTIN MITTELSTADT**, professor of
New Testament, Evangel University

"This book is the testimony of a Pentecostal pastor who worked hard to revitalize the worship of his congregation and, in the process, resuscitated a dying church. Lear writes to other Pentecostals to demonstrate how a church's worship shapes the quality of their discipleship. Some may be uncomfortable with his testimony as it includes historic Christian practices rarely seen in Pentecostal gatherings. You do not have to embrace all his recommendations to appreciate his approach. Lear takes seriously the worship of the church as a faithful response to the full gospel of Jesus under the direction of the Holy Spirit. What could be more Pentecostal than that?"

—**D. ALLEN TENNISON**, theological counsel,
National Office of the Assemblies of God

"*Resurrecting Worship* tells a story we need to hear—how congregations are revitalized in today's culture. My approach to leadership in my own local church has been indelibly impacted by Joseph Lear's reflections. Grounded in the Pentecostal tradition but applicable across Christian denominations, this book offers more than a road map for numerical renewal; it invites Christians into a deeper, theologically rich practice of worship. By returning to the essentials of trinitarian, Eucharistic, and Spirit-led liturgy, the author demonstrates how authentic worship not only sustains faith communities but breathes new life into the mission of the church. This is a profound testimony of how faithful, intentional worship can reawaken the church's call to justice, compassion, and discipleship, while pointing the way toward a kingdom-oriented future. Church leaders seeking both spiritual depth and practical guidance will find in these pages hope for a slow burning, yet powerful revival."

—**KEVIN HARGADEN**, director of the Jesuit
Centre for Faith and Justice, Dublin

"In far too many communities, our churches are failing. Too often the answer is to just begin anew with church planting or multisite approaches without serious attention to the reasons why a church fails or perhaps what has been neglected by those tasked with supporting congregations. Joseph Lear is a true pastor and theologian. He has never been satisfied with the status quo or the latest in church growth trends. By focusing on the work of the Holy Spirit to revive not only the hearts and minds of individuals, Lear developed a Pentecostal liturgy that expanded the spiritual imagination of a community for more than just themselves. This book is a treasure for pastors who are looking for more than strategies, but for a revival of hearts for the work of God in our communities. This is a must read for all leaders who long for real and sustained revival."

—JOY E. A. QUALLS, associate professor, Division of Communication, and associate dean, School of Fine Arts and Communication, Biola University

Resurrecting Worship

A Pentecostal Liturgy For Slow Burn Revival

Joseph M. Lear

Foreword by Chris E. W. Green

CASCADE *Books* • Eugene, Oregon

RESURRECTING WORSHIP
A Pentecostal Liturgy For Slow Burn Revival

Copyright © 2025 Joseph M. Lear. All rights reserved. Except for brief quotations in critical publications or reviews, no part of this book may be reproduced in any manner without prior written permission from the publisher. Write: Permissions, Wipf and Stock Publishers, 199 W. 8th Ave., Suite 3, Eugene, OR 97401.

Cascade Books
An Imprint of Wipf and Stock Publishers
199 W. 8th Ave., Suite 3
Eugene, OR 97401

www.wipfandstock.com

PAPERBACK ISBN: 979-8-3852-0263-8
HARDCOVER ISBN: 979-8-3852-0264-5
EBOOK ISBN: 979-8-3852-0265-2

Cataloguing-in-Publication data:

Names: Lear, Joseph M., author. | Green, Chris E. W., foreword.

Title: Resurrecting worship : a pentecostal liturgy for slow burn revival / Joseph M Lear.

Description: Eugene, OR: Cascade Books, 2025 | Includes bibliographical references.

Identifiers: ISBN 979-8-3852-0263-8 (paperback) | ISBN 979-8-3852-0264-5 (hardcover) | ISBN 979-8-3852-0265-2 (ebook)

Subjects: LCSH: Liturgics | Pentecostal churches—United States—Liturgy |

Classification: BV176 L40 2025 (paperback) | BV176 (ebook)

VERSION NUMBER 01/30/25

For the Assemblies of God.

Go to the nearest smallest church and commit yourself to being there for six months. If it doesn't work out, find somewhere else. But don't look for programs, don't look for entertainment, and don't look for a great preacher. A Christian congregation is not a glamorous place, not a romantic place.

—EUGENE PETERSON

Contents

Foreword

J aroslav Pelikan famously distinguished tradition—"the living faith of the dead," he called it—from traditional*ism*—"the dead faith of the living."[1] I believe revival can be distinguished from revivalism in the same way. The former renews living faith in God for the sake of God's mission, breathing new life into our dead works. The latter chases the feeling of an old experience, seeking to return to the past by imitating, and at times caricaturing, not the works of the saints but what we have come to esteem as their achievements. Revival, in other words, opens us to Christ and the many futures the Spirit makes possible. Revivalism fixates on miraculous interventions, causing us to obsess about ways of manufacturing the particular outcomes we crave.

In the final chapter of this book, Joseph draws a similar distinction. He acknowledges that the move of God sometimes comes raging and consuming, like the fire that blazed on Elijah's altar on Mt. Carmel (1 Kgs 18:38). What we need in this moment, however, is a "slow-burn revival," one that burns like the charcoal Jesus used to cook bread and fish for his disciples (John 21:9). We need this slow-burn revival because revivalism has consumed us and left us burnt out. As Florian Simatupang notes in his forthcoming book, *The Eucharistic Spirit*, we're all of us suffering from a profound spiritual fatigue, the fallout from working for years and

---

1. Pelikan, *Vindication of Tradition*, 65.

years under the unrelenting pressure to produce and reproduce life-altering church services and altar-call experiences.[2]

I am glad that Joseph has written this book and that he is publishing it now. We need it, more than ever. The challenges he urges us to face are not new, of course. And so far, at least, we have not learned the lesson the Spirit has been trying to teach us. In the early 1970s, Walter Hollenweger observed that "a service of the Lord's Supper, in the course of which there is room for the gifts of the Spirit in a Pentecostal assembly, faces the older Pentecostal denominations with liturgical problems which are not easy to solve." To prove his point, he quotes the words of Donald Gee, "the apostle of balance," written thirty years prior:

> Sometimes we hear it suggested that the Breaking of Bread service must be left quite "open": That in it there ought to be no set preaching by the pastor; that there must be no intercession, but only what is called "worship," etc. The result of all this mere traditionalism is to produce meetings so stereotyped that, for all their boasted freedom, they become more barren than the very liturgical services they deprecate—and with less aesthetic appeal . . .[3]

Joseph, like Gee and other early Pentecostals, talks about our worship as a communal and congregational practice—something manifest, embodied, and so shared for the sake of the world. This will leave many shocked, I'm afraid, because most of us have learned to think of worship not as the work the people of God do as the gathered body of Christ but as something the individual feels and expresses with feeling toward a Christ who remains mostly absent and inactive.

Immediately after citing Gee's warnings against traditionalism, Hollenweger describes Pentecostal eucharistic devotion as a form of blood and wounds mysticism, a mysticism marked, he says, by "love for the faithful friend who is called Jesus," an "absorption" into his sufferings, and a "looking forward to the coming

2. Simatupang, *Eucharist Spirit.*
3. Hollenweger, *Pentecostals*, 387.

marriage feast." That seems exactly right to me—and not only as a historical description. What has come to be called the Pentecostal movement is, I believe, a renewal movement, one intended to bring all the faithful back to the altar and to the altering work of the Spirit who flows like a fountain from the wounds of the exalted Christ. The problem is, many of our churches no longer remember how to find those wells, and so cannot drink from them. The liturgy should light the way for us, and those ordained to lead our worship should be trained and prepared to help us follow it. But, as Joseph points out, the oversimplified structure—songs, offering, sermon, and dismissal—that most of our churches follow does not find its genesis in Israel's calling nor its fulfillment in John's apocalyptic vision. And that means our worship cannot be truly lively or life-giving, at least not over the long haul, even if it is energetic.

A friend recently remarked to me that revivalism and traditionalism often involve an unquestioning, unreflective attachment to past experiences. These "isms" are nostalgic, not anamnestic. They are fixated on the past and determined to conform the future to that image; therefore, they have a drastically narrowed focus and a forced perspective. They cannot help us "remember" as we are commanded to do. Faith, by contrast, is open to anything God brings and everything God makes of whatever may come. So, whereas the spirit of revivalism says, "Make this happen," the spirit of revival says, "Let it be with me according to your word" (Luke 1:38).

Our own experience repeatedly confirms it, as do the teachings of the mothers and fathers of the church, including the founders of our own movement: nothing stifles the Spirit more than our attempts to stir the Spirit up. Our attempts to achieve "the pure working of the Spirit" actually only poison the atmosphere. Sharply put, the harder we try to be "Pentecostal," the narrower our focus becomes and the more forced our perspective. All to say, then, I believe the most important words in Joseph's book are right there on the cover. He is calling not for a revitalization of worship but its *resurrection*. That difference makes all the difference, I believe, because resurrection, unlike revitalization, is not something we can do for ourselves, however hard we try. All we can do is keep showing up at the altar, putting our bodies where Christ said he would be present, focusing our attention on the truth of the Scriptures that reveal his goodness to us, holding in our hearts the beauty of his sacred heart and the immaculate heart of his mother.

Acknowledgments

Thank you to my wife, Holly Lear, who told me in the Spirit to write this book. And to Abby Anderson who was a second witness.

Thank you to the congregation of Resurrection Assembly, many of whom have come and gone, for believing with me that God raises the dead.

Resurrecting Liturgy

First Assembly of God in Iowa City was in a bad place. At the beginning of 2016, the church had been without a lead pastor for almost a year. Money was draining from the bank account. The sanctuary carpet had been installed in 1980. Longtime congregants had left out of frustration and disillusionment. With the very real possibility of closing permanently, the church voted to dissolve its board and release control of the church to the Iowa Ministry Network of the Assemblies of God in exchange for an injection of funds. It was declared a church revitalization. As part of this plan, the Iowa Ministry Network reserved the right to appoint the next lead pastor.

They chose me.

The church was in a bad place, but the kingdom of God was present. The one ministry that was vibrant, growing, and making a significant impact on the community was the kids and youth ministry. Every Wednesday and Sunday, Pastor Abby Anderson would host neighborhood kids for worship and church family meals. She had grown up in the church as what the public school called an "at-risk" kid herself. With little to no money to work with, Pastor Abby was living the Lord's Prayer from week to week. She was teaching the kids to pray, "Give us today our daily bread," and would then cobble together a meal for thirty to forty hungry kids.

The church is located less than two miles from the University of Iowa campus. When I was appointed in January 2016, I imagined that I would be part of what some might call a "university church." I was fresh out of a doctoral program in New Testament, and I wanted to pastor in an academic community. Iowa City seemed a like great fit. In the first two years of my pastorate, I was also the Chi Alpha Christian Ministries campus pastor at the U. But the church never became a hangout only for the academic elite. To this day, it's a haven for the poor and the hungry.

. . .

Churches in North America face an uncertain future. Each year more churches are closing their doors permanently. A 2021 report from Lifeway Research details that Protestant churches are losing a net 1,500 congregations per year.[1] In other words, the church in America is in a bad place. Seventy percent of churches have an average weekly attendance of under a hundred people, which means that should nearly three-quarters of the churches in America lose a few families, they'd face a financial, volunteer, and lay leadership crisis.[2]

This book is proof, however, that God is not done with the small church. The blazing fires of newly founded churches, national growth, and church planting have been squelched, but the coals are still burning. The Spirit of God is still in the burning bushes scattered across the American landscape. The kingdom of God is still present, which means there's a path forward for renewal. It's not going to come with marketing campaigns and managerial ingenuity. It's going to come when small congregations get back to the basics of worshipping in Spirit and truth. We need a slow burn revival.

1. Earls, "Protestant Church Closures."
2. Earls, "Small Churches."

. . .

The First Assembly is now called Resurrection Assembly of God. The name change signifies not only what God has done in our midst. God has of course raised the church out of a place of near death. But the church's name also declares the very reason the church itself exists. The reason Resurrection Assembly feeds hungry kids, the reason we advocate for the homeless and housing-insecure, the reason we help immigrants and refugees navigate an impossibly bureaucratic border, the reason we live graciously with the drug- and alcohol-addicted, and the reason the disabled lead from the pulpit—the reason we do all of these things is because we worship the risen Lord, Jesus Christ.

While some of our ministries seem easily to align with the so-called "woke" opinions of the educated elite, we do not attempt to prove ourselves to the politically liberal-majority community of Iowa City. Rather, we confess and proclaim the resurrection of the dead and the life of the world to come. On the day of Pentecost, the Spirit was poured out and the disciples spoke in other tongues. Peter proclaimed "these are the last days" (Acts 2:17) and said this was the case because Jesus had been raised from the dead. As a result, the Jerusalem church had "all things common" as they gathered "in gladness and singleness of heart worshipping God" (Acts 2:44–47).[3] The book of Acts, not the shallowness of American politics, is our reason for being.

The title of this book has a double meaning. In the first instance, this book is about the "resurrection" of dead worship. It is the story of the Spirit bringing the dead practices of the church back to life. The second meaning is grounded in the Pentecostal experience of the earliest church in Acts. We want to worship the way people who are expecting to be resurrected on the Last Day ought to worship. These are the last days: let us therefore gather with gladness and singleness of heart to worship the resurrected Lord. Everything we do must flow from that.

---

3. All Scripture translations in this book are my own.

. . .

It's now 2024 and the church is now out of the revitalization process. We have our own governing board of deacons, and we are continuing in the work of the gospel. We still have to pray for our daily bread, but the prospect of closing the church is no longer on anyone's radar. How did we get here?

Abby and I formed an instant partnership. Unbeknownst to us, we had both attended Central Bible College (now Evangel University) in Springfield, Missouri at the same time. But we did not meet until I showed up in Iowa City. It was and is a partnership that can only be attributed to the Holy Spirit. In a church movement that puts so much emphasis on CEO-style church leadership, we were united in our conviction that the path to a revitalized church was the path of revitalized worship.

The word "worship" in Pentecostal (and evangelical) circles is often used in the thinnest sense possible of "singing songs together." That is not what I am talking about. When I use the word "worship" I am talking about the whole of the church's formal gathering time, from songs to prayer to preaching to the communion altar. I am talking about liturgy.

The word "liturgy" risks conjuring some unhelpful associations, and it is a word that is alien to my Pentecostal movement. On the one hand, it might bring to mind (however unfairly) overly formalized, rigid, un-Spirited church tradition. On the other hand, it might bring to mind (again, however unfairly) the implementation of call-and-response forms of worship that some emerging churches practice to be different (for the sake of difference?), or to put an intellectual spin on worship. These associations are both unhelpful. The word "liturgy" itself could use somewhat of a resurrection in (so-called) nonliturgical churches. Liturgy, let us say for now, is simply intentional, biblical, trinitarian worship.

Here is a fact that churches need to wrestle with: everyone has a liturgy. In evangelical circles, it is typically described as an "order of service," but it's a liturgy nevertheless. Every Pentecostal (and evangelical) church I have been to has an order of service that looks more or less like this:

- Three to five songs
- Prayer
- Offering and announcements
- Sermon
- Closing prayer

There is nothing wrong with this. But there is no obvious reason for it either. Certainly there is no biblical basis for it.

It seems that certain patterns of worship have taken on an authoritative status. They have become Tradition with a capital "T." This has, of course, not happened because there is a hierarchical church structure demanding it. And, to be honest, I am not sure why this pattern of worship has so taken hold. It seems that it is in part fueled by pragmatism: It works. People keep coming. But good attendance is by no means a biblical measure for right worship.

Abby and I began asking ourselves, "What is right worship of the triune God?" In other words, we wanted to cultivate formational worship—the kind of worship that forms Christian disciples over the long haul. We wanted our worship to be a cohesive whole, not simply what others had cobbled together for reasons no longer available to us. Cohesion is something we knew historic church traditions had in mind when they had formed their liturgies, and we wanted to follow in their footsteps—applying their ancient wisdom to our contemporary circumstances. We wanted to follow them not only in content (i.e., that God is Trinity and needs to be worshipped as such), but also in form. How do we do everything in our church life, beginning with Sunday morning worship, in such a way that makes committed disciples of the God in whose name—Father, Son, and Holy Spirit—we are all baptized?

We, of course, by no means rejected pragmatic solutions to pragmatic problems at the church. We had to implement new kinds of managerial systems, we had to hire some new people, and we had to market the church's renewal to the community. We changed the carpet! But we never believed that any amount of managerial ingenuity would produce a revitalized church. For this church to be raised from near death, we needed to resurrect worship. And we needed resurrecting worship—the kind of worship that prepares the church for the resurrection of the dead and the life of the world to come.

This book is not a 1–2–3, step-by-step process to revitalizing a local church. When someone suggests there are clearly defined processes (especially in managerial terms) that can be followed to revitalizing a church, they have either never done it themselves or they have misinterpreted their own experience. Rather, this book is what we call in Pentecostal circles a "testimony." It is a narrative of the work of God in very particular circumstances. We made it our aim to worship God rightly in everything we did, and God has given our church new life. My hope is that, by narrating the revitalization of Resurrection Assembly of God, God will be not only glorified, but also that our story will inspire other churches who, regardless of their financial situation or numerical attendance, also need resurrecting worship.

. . .

I need to say it again: *Resurrecting Worship* is not a how-to for revitalizing a church. Rather, it is a biblical pattern set out in the Scriptures. And the task of the church is to be biblically faithful. "Bless the Lord, my soul, and all that is within me, bless his holy name!" (Ps 103:1). The Psalmist is convinced that the only response to God's forgiveness of sins, the healing of sickness, the deliverance from death (vv. 2–4) is worship. When the Israelites see the Egyptians drowned, they worship: "I will sing to the Lord, because he has triumphed triumphantly" (Exod 15:1). When Jesus meets the woman at the well, she disputes where God's people are to worship, but what she assumes should not go unnoted: The task given to the people of God is indeed to worship (John 4:20). Paul says offering our bodies as living sacrifices is our spiritual act of worship (Rom 12:1). The author of Hebrews invites the church to "worship God acceptably, with reverence and awe" (Heb 12:28). When John falls down to worship the angel at the end of his revelations, the angel stops him with the injunction, "Worship God!" (Rev 22:9). The biblical witness does not see worship as a single item in the Christian to-do list. The church's life is quite simply to worship.

At Resurrection Assembly, we realized that if we took worship seriously, we could only succeed in our task. We could only succeed because when a church makes its sole purpose to worship God intentionally, rightly, and biblically, whether the church remains open or closes becomes a moot point.

Viability is not everything. This is another conviction that runs against the grain of so much of the church's understanding of success in the Western world, particularly in the United States. Every year the Assemblies of God asks me to fill out an annual church ministries report. It is a census of sorts for the fellowship: how many people attend? How many people converted? How many were baptized? What is the racial make-up of your church? The fellowship also hands out regular awards for top missions-giving churches. Churches with explosive numerical growth always make the headlines. Success in the American church—as in America generally speaking—is measured numerically.

But that is not what we see in the Bible. For sure, there is a book of the Bible called "Numbers" in which the people of God are counted. But we also have to remember that David and Israel were punished for taking a census (see 1 Chr 21). Counting is not intrinsically wrong, but it cannot—biblically speaking—be the sole measure of success. Paul's missionary work in the book of Acts was of course to gain converts, but his journeys are replete with stories that modern American sensibilities might erroneously categorize as failure. The apostle Paul had to at times shake the dust off his feet against a town (Acts 13:51), but there is no indication that Paul understood that as a defeat for the gospel.

Jesus himself seemed to believe numbers are not everything. When John the Baptist's disciples asked Jesus if they should look for another or if he was in fact the real deal, he cited miracles, not numbers: "the dead are raised, the poor have good news preached to them" (Luke 7:22). And Jesus died. As he was crucified, he said, "not my will but let yours be done" (Luke 22:42). In the world's eyes, death is always chalked up as a defeat. But God is the God of resurrection. We were convinced that as long as we were worshipping the God of resurrection, whether the church lived or died, God's resurrecting power would not let our spiritual act of worship be a failure in kingdom terms. The church could "die" by permanently closing the doors of the building. But such a death might in the end make us all the more like the risen Lord we worship.

The conviction that success in kingdom terms is not in the numbers alone also comes from my Pentecostal discipleship, which itself was biblically grounded. The Bible is a story, and my Pentecostal catechesis always taught me that proof of God's presence is in the story, not in a list of objective facts and figures. Again, this is why this book is written as testimony. We have seen a numerical increase at Resurrection Assembly of God, but the proof of God's presence is in the story—both in the day to day, mundane miracles of home visitations, and in the overarching narrative that God has seen fit to raise this church up as it has worshipped his name in word and deed.

. . .

I have already said that we wanted our worship to be biblical. That means we wanted to have scriptural basis for everything we did. We did our best to take the whole of the biblical witness into account, and perform worship accordingly. Having said that, two caveats about "biblical worship" are in order. First of all, as the leadership of Resurrection Assembly, knew we were not sufficient for this task, so we approached it with fear and trembling. We could not make the audacious claim to have faithfully digested the whole of the Bible and so have "biblical worship." One of the most significant ways we dealt with this insufficiency was by listening to the voices of the historic church. As the book of Hebrews says, we are surrounded by a great cloud of witnesses (Heb 12:1). With God's help, we have listened to them, and we continue to do so.

The second caveat is this: I know that the modifier "biblical" is put in front of just about anything that an American evangelical wants to validate. The word has been used so liberally and in so many contexts that it demands some guardrails. Some people—for example—think it is biblical to have women wear doily-style head-coverings and to handle snakes in worship. We had three guardrails: worship had to be trinitarian, eucharistic, and Pentecostal. These words provide a helpful taxonomy for narrating our intentions throughout the yearslong revitalization. They therefore provide the chapter titles of this book, and so deserve brief introduction.

First, we wanted our worship to be trinitarian. To the extent that the Bible is the written revelation of the one God who is Father, Son, and Holy Spirit, our worship needed to be explicitly trinitarian. The reality of my Pentecostal upbringing was that I knew I was a trinitarian Christian, but I always categorized this as an intellectual item we held in books and propositional documents. At Resurrection, we realized that the witness of the church going back to the New Testament did not relegate trinitarian confession to a matter of mental assent. It was in fact confession, and therefore it was something to be performed in corporate confession and song, in kneeling together in reverence, and in eating the Lord's Supper. We did not want anyone to leave our church not knowing the God we worship is one in three and three in one. We are in fact baptized into the name of the Father, Son, and Holy Spirit. Our trinitarian performance must not end with a dunk in our church's Iowan horse trough.

Second, we wanted eucharistic worship. "Eucharist" is simply a word for the Lord's Supper coming from the ancient Greek for "giving thanks." Jesus declared that this was his new covenant with the church before he died. He also said, "do this!" And we wanted to take Jesus's words seriously. Ancient Israel's entire life centered on the covenant God made with them by bringing them out of Egypt with the Passover. We were compelled to follow their pattern. Still, we wanted to do this not only on biblical grounds, which means it is intrinsically right to do, but also because of the formative power the Supper presents. We wanted people to be formed as disciples who would lay down their lives for others just as their Lord did for them.

Third, we wanted Pentecostal worship. This requires a little more explanation than the first two modifiers. We by no means wanted people only to speak in tongues—though we clearly celebrated any genuine move of the Spirit in the church. The conviction, as I have already said, was that Pentecostal worship is biblical worship. At root, this is based on the outpouring of the Holy Spirit at the beginning of the book of Acts. The church is only the church performing trinitarian and eucharistic worship if indeed it is the Pentecostal church. The Spirit's outpouring created an eschatological—an end-times—people who are no longer defined by race, gender, or class, but by the Spirit who has anointed them. As Paul himself says, "there is neither Jew nor Greek; there is neither slave nor free; there is neither male nor female" (Gal 3:28).

If the Pentecostal church is defined by the Spirit, not the categories of the present age, then we decided that we needed to expect that our church would be made up of the same racial and class diversity that was reflected in Iowa City (and, of course, that there would be both male and female). We knew we should not only expect it, but we needed to implement practices that would open the door for the Spirit to move in that way. So, for example, our conviction was that worship is a performance, and that it is not performed only by those who stand at the altar or behind the pulpit. The stage of our worship is the entire church. There are no spectators. We therefore invited those in the pews to participate and to participate as they were. Women and men. Children and the elderly. The poor and (sometimes) the rich. On the feast of Pentecost 2019, we invited everyone who could pray in another language to pray the Lord's prayer. We prayed in fifteen different languages, and that with an attendance of only about seventy-five people. We did not have a contrived multiculturalism, it was simply and forthrightly the unity of the Spirit that held us together in worship.

Pentecostal worship is also emphatically eschatological worship. On the day of Pentecost, the apostle Peter said, "these are the last days" (Acts 2:17). And so in order for worship to be biblically Pentecostal, it had to be eschatological. This has come out most explicitly in the act of preaching. No matter the passage of the Bible that is the sermon's text, we made every effort to show the Scripture's eschatological meaning. We are Spirit-anointed people who await a King and his kingdom. Every virtue, every command, every meditation, and every thought must be taken captive by that reality. Church begins with the call to worship: "Blessed be God: Father, Son, and Holy Spirit; blessed be God forever." From there we sing of the coming kingdom. We proclaim its nearness as we open the Scriptures. And we set our hearts on it at the conclusion of the eucharistic prayer when we ask God to bring us, with all of the church, into the joy of his eternal kingdom.

. . .

Finally, a word on who this book is for. I have already made repeated reference to my own Pentecostal tradition, and to the broader evangelical church that (at least historically white-majority) Pentecostalism has been at times associated with. My own Pentecostal tradition, including its pastors, leaders, and laypeople, is my primary audience. But others will find this book helpful as they seek to revitalize worship and connect their worship to the works of justice the church is called to. Evangelicals will find in these pages a critical appraisal of their pragmatism and reliance on cutting-edge marketplace techniques. However, I believe evangelicals also have a sincere desire to see God's kingdom come, and so they will discover in this book the tools necessary to rethink the very things the Spirit has without a doubt already been telling them to rethink. Still yet, this book will provide a fresh perspective for historic protestant traditions—Methodists, Presbyterians, and Episcopalians to name a few—who struggle to connect their liturgy to the works of justice they so desperately want execute.

Resurrection Assembly of God is the story of a slow burn revival. It started with the Pentecostal liturgy contained in the pages below. It's a pattern of worship that renewed, motivated, and sustained a church that sees kid-friendly potlucks, the welcoming of the immigrant, and the cancellation of debts. The challenge in this testimony is for other churches to see what the Spirit is doing, and fan the flame of the gifts God has given.

Questions for Reflection and Discussion

1. Prayerfully consider where the kingdom of God is present in your church. How can you tell? Write all of this in a clear, concise paragraph (or two) that could be put in a bulletin or on a big screen to present to the church.

2. Write out your order of service. Is there biblical basis for each part of your liturgy? If so, write it down. Is your church aware of the biblical basis for your weekly liturgy?

3. If you were to reimagine a liturgy for your church from the ground up, what would it look like? Write out every movement of the service, and its biblical basis.

Trinitarian Worship

"Blessed be God," I say to the church. The church repeats. And then I add, "Father, Son, and Holy Spirit." The church repeats again. This is how we begin every Sunday's communion service. When we end communion, we address the Father: "To Jesus Christ, to you, and to the Holy Spirit be honor and glory forever and ever." From the very first moments of our gathering to the very last, we confess and worship God as Trinity.

We also always conclude our Sunday morning worship by singing the Doxology:

> Praise God from whom all blessings flow,
> Praise him all creatures here below,
> Praise him above ye heavenly host,
> Praise Father, Son, and Holy Ghost.

One of our members once expressed the tremendous comfort singing praise to God: Father, Son, and Holy Spirit brings her. She described singing this song as a "big hug." This is exactly what trinitarian worship is supposed to be. The Trinity is not a matter only of the brain, the intellect. The trinitarian God envelopes all of creation. He takes not just our thoughts, but our bodies and our emotions—all that we are as his people—into his divine embrace. As we kiss the Son (Ps 2:12), we are held by the Holy Spirit, who is the Comforter, the Embrace of the Father (John 14:26).

Biblical worship is trinitarian worship because the story of the Bible is the story of the trinitarian God. God the Father created the heavens and the earth. Jesus Christ, the Son of God, became incarnate of the virgin Mary and was publicly revealed as the Son at his baptism. The Holy Spirit was poured out on Pentecost. The Father creates. The Son redeems. The Holy Spirit restores.

Each of those events in themselves is also narrated in a trinitarian fashion. God the Father spoke creation into being as the "Spirit of God was hovering over the face of the deep" (Gen 1:2). By Jesus, the Son, "all things were created" (Col 1:16). When Jesus is revealed as the Son of God at his baptism, the entire Godhead is revealed. God the Father spoke to the Son as the Spirit descended on him like a dove. Pentecost is no different. Peter says the Spirit is poured out because Jesus, the Son, has been exalted to the right hand of the Father (Acts 2:33). If God has revealed himself as Trinity, and reveals himself in a trinitarian fashion every time he does, then we must of course worship him accordingly. God's story as Trinity should be the story of every church gathering. I knew that if we wanted to see God bring new life to our church, then we needed to start here.

As I said in the introduction to this book, all of our worship is oriented by the church's confession of God as Trinity. But there are three facets of our worship that we could meaningfully say flow most immediately from our trinitarian confession: Baptism, the creeds, and corporate prayer. I will take up each of these matters in this chapter, narrating how they are indispensable elements in our Pentecostal liturgy. The following two chapters will, in turn, show how these all flow from one another and result in worship that is also eucharistic and Pentecostal.

Baptism

Baptism is nothing unless it is trinitarian. It is literally just splashing in water with clothes on unless trinitarian words are spoken by the one performing the baptism. And those words must follow Jesus's own command to his disciples after his resurrection: "Go, therefore, make disciples of all nations, baptizing them in the name of the Father and the Son and the Holy Spirit." "Name" in the biblical text is singular. The persons are three. There you not only have a baptismal formula; you also have a beautiful, simple, and sublime account of the Trinity.

Jesus's command to us is to make disciples. If we were going to see our church revitalized, we knew we needed to obey our Lord. Baptizing is where discipleship begins. So we set out to make sure that everyone in our church who claimed Christ with their lips was baptized. However, we didn't want to stop with the event of baptism itself. We wanted our congregation to live the baptized life.

There is a case to be made that baptism is simply what the Christian life is all about. Theologian Robert Jenson has said that the entirety of the Christian life is simply coming back to our baptisms.[1] Michael Budde has said that, as Christians, baptism is our "primary and formative" identity.[2] In other words, our baptisms trump everything else about us. Before we are male or female, American or Congolese, living in suburbia or in Section 8 housing, we are baptized. Not only that, it is also an identity that we live into. It should be our meditation—the life event we always come back to in order to understand who we are. From the pulpit, I compare it to a marriage or a citizenship ceremony. It is a public ceremony in which you claim and are claimed by another, and your loyalty must therefore be given from then onward. After all, Paul doesn't say we are all one in Christ because we have claimed Jesus with our lips—though that is obviously a necessary component. He claims we are all one in Christ because we have all been baptized into him (Gal 3:27).

If it is true that we are all in Christ because we are baptized, that raises a couple of questions. The first is theological: In what way does baptism mean that we are "in Christ" as Paul says in Galatians? One of our main tasks at Resurrection has been to unpack

1. Jenson, *Systematic Theology*, 297.
2. Budde, *Borders of Baptism*, 3.

how we are "in Christ" through baptism precisely so people can see how to live the baptized life. I will show some of the ways we have done that. The second is more practical, but has everything to do with the liturgy of our communal gatherings: How did we bring baptism into every church service when there weren't necessarily people to baptize every Sunday?

. . .

I say from the pulpit that if we want to know what is happening in Christian baptism, we need only look at Jesus's experience. I already described it above. It's a trinitarian event: When Jesus comes out of the water, God the Father says, "This is my beloved Son," and as he says it, the Holy Spirit descends on him in the form of a dove.[3] The same is true for us. When we come up out of the water, God the Father says, "You are my beloved son/daughter," and the Holy Spirit descends on us like a dove. Ordinary senses don't suffice. But we can see and hear what is truly happening in the Spirit.

However, it is not as if our baptisms are merely parallel to Jesus's. They are not two separate instances of a reiterating event. The reason we can say our baptisms look just like Jesus's baptism is because his baptism is our baptism. Paul says it plainly in 1 Cor 12:13, "for in one Spirit, we were all baptized into one body," and that body is Christ's. If we are in his body, then whatever is true of him, must also be true of us. I have told the church to think of it as a Spirit-enabled time-warp—something that happens repeatedly in the Bible. Ezekiel can be lifted up in the Spirit and transferred from the river Chebar in exile to the east gate of Jerusalem (Ezek 11:1). Paul could be absent in body, but present in spirit to the Corinthian church (1 Cor 5:3). John, the author of Revelation, can be carried away to a wilderness where he sees Babylon the Great (Rev 17:3). In a similar way, all of us are in Christ at the Jordan River in our baptisms despite the separation of time and space.

3. Matt 3:13–17; Mark 1:9–11; Luke 3:21–22.

"For as many as have been baptized into Christ, have put on Christ" (Gal 3:27). Again, whatever is true of Christ must be true of us. I have often said from the pulpit that the only discernible difference between the church and Christ is that we are still sinful. It is a significant difference, but a difference only highlighted by how closely Christ and his church are identified in the New Testament.

The Scriptures say we are in Christ not only about the past, but about future events as well. Paul says that because we have been baptized into Christ, we have not only been crucified and buried with him in death, we are also guaranteed to be united with him in a resurrection like his (Rom 6:4–6). We are promised resurrection because we are in Christ through baptism. But the future is not merely in the future. Think of the Spirit's time-warp again. Paul says that because we will be resurrected in Christ, we can walk in newness of life now (Rom 6:4). That newness is not artificial. In a sense, we are already living resurrected lives because we have been baptized into Christ and Christ has already been raised from the dead. In Christ, we live Christ's life. This is what Paul is ultimately getting at when he says "to live is Christ" (Phil 1:21).

· · ·

What I have said so far only begins to get at what it means to make our baptized lives the event we always come back to and what it means to make it our "primary and formative identity." The whole of the New Testament might be said to be a working out of what it means simply to be "in Christ." But there is one more aspect of what it means to be baptized and therefore "in Christ" that threads its way through the New Testament and is therefore important to highlight. The New Testament says that to be in Christ is to be a member of the body of Christ. That is, the words "in Christ" apply to the church first and foremost as a corporate body.

Another thing I regularly say from the pulpit is that we cannot be Christians by ourselves. Israel in the Old Testament was not a loosely connected group of like-minded individuals who got together on a semi-regular basis to offer their individual sacrifices.

On the contrary, they were a people with a common story. They were not individually saved from slavery in Egypt to make their personal journeys to the promised land. They all passed through the Red Sea together. They were all liberated together, and the Passover was eaten together on the same day—a national holy day—from then on. The same is true of the church. To be sure, we are all individually baptized, but we are baptized into the baptized people who are all one in Christ. Paul calls the Red Sea and the cloud Israel's baptism (1 Cor 10:1–2), and in that way he tells the church that they all might have been baptized individually, but they are baptized in the same sanctified water and in the same Holy Spirit.

Paul says, "for in one Spirit we were all baptized into one body" (1 Cor 12:13). Again, this is not artificial. It is not simply a way of speaking. Paul thinks the corporate body of Christ is just as much a body as the one his own two legs are standing on is. He goes on: "For the body is not one member but many" (1 Cor 12:14). From there, Paul speaks of the different roles each individual plays in the body of Christ. Some are eyes, some are hands, some are feet. No member of the body lacks honor, because every part has a role to play to make it a functioning body (1 Cor 12:15–31).

To help us understand just how much Paul thinks his use of the word "body" is analogous to any individual's body, we can look to an earlier passage in 1 Corinthians that assumes what Paul says about the oneness of the baptized church. In 1 Cor 6:12–20, Paul urges the church to flee sexual immorality. He challenges the congregation to take the Genesis narrative seriously, which says that two become one flesh when they are united sexually (1 Cor 6:16; cf. Gen 2:24). Up until this point, it may seem as if Paul is only talking to the individuals in the congregation, telling each of them, individually, not to have sex with people they are not married to. But in 6:19, Paul uses the plural "you" when he says, "do you not know that your body is the temple of the Holy Spirit?" In English, we use the word "you" to refer both to an individual and to a group of people. In some places in the USA, the singular and plural uses are differentiated with the word "y'all." If we were to adopt that terminology, we could translate 1 Cor 6:19 as "don't y'all know that y'all's body is the temple of the Holy Spirit?" The word "you" is plural, but the word "body" is singular in 1 Cor 6:19. The church, though many members, is one body. And he doesn't say, as it is often said in evangelical culture, that each individual body is a temple. He says the church body is the temple of the Holy Spirit. The implication of what Paul is saying here will be shocking to most people who have grown up in the West where we are falsely taught that only individuals have bodies. Paul is saying that when you enter a brothel, you are involving the whole church with the prostitute in the sexual act.

In sum, the baptism is the trinitarian event that constitutes the church. It is why the New Testament says we are "in Christ," and therefore one body. And this has both positive and negative ramifications. Positively, we are the temple of the Holy Spirit, and we all have a role to play in the resurrected body. Negatively, when we sin, this affects not just our personal lives, but the life of the whole church. With all of this in view, baptism is clearly foundational for the church's sense of who it is as the Trinity-worshipping church. The question we must now move onto is, "how did we, through the liturgy of the service, make baptism, and therefore the Trinity, our 'primary and formative' identity?"

The Creeds

The Christian creeds—both the Apostles' and the Nicene—are one of the main ways we make baptism our primary and formative identity. We prepare individuals for baptism by teaching them, among other things, these ancient Christian creeds. The creeds are trinitarian. They begin with a confession of God the Father, creator of heaven and earth. They move on to Jesus Christ the Risen Lord. And they conclude with confessing the Holy Spirit who constitutes God's holy church. This part of baptismal preparation is a cornerstone of the church's trinitarian worship.

This is the process we follow for those wanting to be baptized. First, we find them a sponsor who will attend all baptismal preparations with them. The sponsor will also stand with them and pray for them right before we baptize. The reasons we have sponsors are several. But one of the practical reasons is that we have seen far too many people go through our baptismal teachings, get baptized, and then never come back to the church again. Having a sponsor to walk through the whole process with them also means that, from the beginning, they realize baptism isn't just about them. It is about the church welcoming them into the body of Christ. It also means that there will be another Christian following up with them post-baptism, to help them work out their salvation with fear and trembling.

The baptism teachings are threefold. We teach basic prayer through the use of the Lord's Prayer. We teach basic Christian morality of the love of God and neighbor through the Ten Commandments. And, like I have said, we teach them the ancient Christian creeds. The creed is the foundation of the baptismal promises the person getting baptized makes right before getting in the water. I ask them, before the whole congregation, "Do you believe in God the Father?" The congregation is then invited to affirm their belief with the person getting baptized by saying, "I do." The same words are followed for the Son and the Holy Spirit. In this moment, the person getting baptized makes a public declaration of his or her belief in God as Trinity. But, just as important, the church reaffirms, corporately, her own baptismal vows in remembrance of when they were each individually born of water and the Spirit.

To make baptism a weekly remembrance, we recite the Nicene Creed (or, sometimes, depending on the occasion, the Apostles' Creed) as a congregation. The person in charge of leading the creed says, "We believe in one God the Father almighty." The congregation repeats. The leader then says, "maker of heaven and earth" before then proclaiming, "And in one Lord Jesus Christ, the only Son of God." The congregation then repeats the line about Jesus. From there, the leader completes reciting the section on Jesus, before saying, "and we believe in the Holy Spirit, the Lord, the Giver of Life." The congregation again repeats before the leader finishes the creed. It is concluded with a resounding congregational "amen."

There is no reason why the congregation couldn't simply recite the whole creed in unison, but we have found that only repeating these three lines helps in particular those who have a learning disability to participate.

Here is what it looks like visually. The bold are the parts the congregation repeats after the leader:

We believe in one God,
    the Father almighty,
        maker of heaven and earth,
        of all things visible and invisible.
And in one Lord Jesus Christ,
    the only Son of God,
        begotten from the Father before all ages,
            God from God,
            Light from Light,
            true God from true God,
        begotten, not made;
        of the same essence as the Father.
        Through him all things were made.
        For us and for our salvation
            he came down from heaven;
            he became incarnate by the Holy Spirit and the virgin Mary,
            and was made human.
            He was crucified for us under Pontius Pilate;
            he suffered and was buried.
            The third day he rose again, according to the Scriptures.
            He ascended to heaven
            and is seated at the right hand of the Father.
            He will come again with glory
            to judge the living and the dead.
            His kingdom will never end.
And we believe in the Holy Spirit,
    the Lord, the giver of life.
        He proceeds from the Father and the Son,
        and with the Father and the Son is worshiped and glorified.
        He spoke through the prophets.
        We believe in one holy worldwide and apostolic church.
        We affirm one baptism for the forgiveness of sins.

We look forward to the resurrection of the dead,
and to life in the world to come.
[*Together*] Amen.

When I was a child, I attended a school that required us to recite the American Pledge of Allegiance before our daily studies started. That pagan practice sheds light on how the creeds function in our church. At times, I even put my hand on my heart as I recite the creeds with the church. It is the grounding confession of all that we do. It is our declaration of independence from every other human institution that would vie for our affection. Before we pray together corporately, before we study the Scriptures, and before we approach the Communion Table, we pledge our allegiance to the one true God: Father, Son, and Holy Spirit.

Prayer

The creed concludes with "amen." Our confession is a prayer, and, as such, it is an entry point into (what we can call) the Divine Conversation Who is God as Trinity. Prayer flows from our confession of God as Trinity, which necessitates that the act of prayer itself is trinitarian in our liturgy. In our order of service, the creed leads us into a time of prayer, which culminates in the corporate act of praying the prayer Jesus himself taught us. To explain why the Lord's Prayer, and with it all of our prayers, are trinitarian in form, we need first to explain how the very act of prayer itself assumes that God is Father, Son, and Holy Spirit.

To see the trinitarian foundations of prayer, we can once again look to baptism, and to Jesus's baptism in particular. Let us rehearse it again. When Jesus was baptized, God the Father spoke: "You are my beloved Son." In doing so, Jesus, as the Son of God, is invited to respond to God the Father as the Son. And indeed we see him doing this. For example, Luke 10:21 records Jesus saying, "I thank you, Father." Coming back to the baptism, we see the Holy Spirit descending in the form of a dove on Jesus when he comes up out of the water. We can therefore say that in baptism, we see (as I said above) the whole Conversation that God is. The Father speaks. The Son responds. The Spirit is the conversing.

To pray is to enter that Divine Conversation. How do we do that? Precisely through our own baptism, which, as I explained above, makes us "in Christ." Through baptism, the church is united with Christ so that we actually speak with Christ to the Father in the Holy Spirit. As an aside, I have often experienced church members wondering if God hears them when they pray. This basic but profound grounding of prayer in God as Trinity provides great comfort to those who might feel like they are just talking to the air. Does God hear us when we pray? Yes, because, through baptism, we are already part of the Conversation.

The Lord's Prayer

This brings us to the prayer Jesus himself taught us to pray. It begins, "Our Father." The reason Jesus invites us to refer to God as Father is precisely because of our baptism. We can only call God Father if we are his sons and daughters. And we can only truly be his children if in fact we are united with his only Son. As Galatians 3:29 says, if we are Christ's then we are "heirs according to the promise." We have entered that trinitarian conversation speaking in the Holy Spirit with Christ to our Father. The Father always hears the Son because they are One in the Spirit. We are therefore guaranteed the same open ear of the Father when we are in Christ.

The plural "our" in the opening address of "our Father" means that this prayer is first and foremost the church's prayer, not the prayer of any one individual. That is why we pray it corporately in our Sunday liturgy. Indeed, the prayer is most fittingly and authentically prayed corporately given that opening word. We of course encourage people to pray it individually in private times of prayer, but saying the word "our" functions as a reminder that this prayer can only be meaningfully prayed in connection with the whole body of Christ.

The Lord's Prayer seems to have fallen into some disrepute amongst evangelicals. This is a most saddening reality. I learned this prayer growing up in the church, but I quickly realized that this was considered by my elders to be a prayer reserved for children. When one grows up—so I was implicitly taught—you speak words that are more authentic. Extemporaneous prayer—where you speak in a stream of consciousness (the more elaborate the better)—is often considered the height of spiritual maturity. It also is thought to be more accessible to the masses.

The fear of inauthentic and vain repetition is, of course, well-founded. Jesus himself warned against it. In Matthew 6:7, Jesus warns us not to "babble on like the Gentiles, for they think that with their many words they will be heard." But we quickly forget that Jesus warns about this right before he says, "pray like this"—after which he recites what we call the Lord's Prayer. What makes us heard is not that we have a bunch of fancy words or that they are off-the-cuff. What makes us heard is that we are co-heirs with Christ and can therefore call God "our Father." Churches everywhere would do better to equip Christians with the profound and simple words of Jesus.

. . .

If we take seriously that Jesus gives us precise words to pray, what becomes clear is that Jesus is against babbling, not repetition. As I have already said, we pray the Lord's prayer corporately every Sunday. But there is also a high degree of repetition in the other matters we pray for during corporate times of prayer.

Because we want trinitarian worship, we seek to make all of our prayers trinitarian in form. With that, we also seek to make all of our prayers profoundly scriptural, drawing on the very words of the Bible to make our prayers to God. We do this not only to be intentional in how we pray together, but also to teach the church how they ought to pray on their own. There are pressing matters of prayer that we focus on from week to week, depending on what is happening in our congregation and in our world. But as a general rule, we pray for the universal and local church, for the United

States of America (since it is the country we live in) and all who are in authority, and for the welfare of the world.

Here is a sampling of some of the prayers we pray with intentional repetition.

Following the lead of the Nicene Creed that confesses one holy worldwide church, we pray for the universal church, its members, and its mission:

> Jesus, You are the Vine, we are the branches. We pray Your church would be one. Holy Spirit, fill the members of Your church. Father, send us out to proclaim the gospel even as You sent Jesus our Lord to proclaim the gospel.

Note the Scriptures invoked. We make Jesus's high priestly prayer from John 17 the foundation of our prayer for the church. The church is highly fragmented not only denominationally, but also within the walls of individual congregations. So, praying for unity builds a foundation for preaching it, enacting it, and calling those who break unity to repent. Asking the Holy Spirit to fill the members of the church hearkens to the Pentecost outpouring in Acts 2. Following the prayer for unity with a supplication for the Holy Spirit to fill us establishes that the Holy Spirit is our Unity. As Ephesians 4:4 says, "There is one body and one Spirit." Finally, when we pray that God would send us, we are remembering some of Jesus's last words to his disciples, "As the Father has sent me, even so, I am sending you" (John 20:21). Unified, the church prays that she can carry out her singular mission.

We also pray for the local church and our city:

> Jesus, may we preach Your gospel in this city. [Here we pray for other local churches by name]. Holy Spirit, give us Yourself that we may use your gifts for the building up of your church. Father, call the people of this city into Your kingdom. May they believe on the Lord Jesus Christ and be baptized that they too might receive the Holy Spirit.

The first line of this prayer follows from the last line of praying for God's universal church in acknowledging that it is in fact

Jesus's gospel that we preach (cf. Mark 1:14–15). In that way, we remind ourselves that we must ever align ourselves with that reality. The prayer for the Holy Spirit to come also follows from praying for the universal church, but in a localized way. Praying for the Holy Spirit himself before praying for his gifts reminds us that, as Paul says, though there are a number of gifts, "to each is given a manifestation of the Spirit for benefit of all" (1 Cor 12:7). This is also why we pray that the gifts he gives us will build up the church (1 Cor 14:12).

In that context, we also pray for particular challenges facing our locality. This often includes praying for the homeless, the housing and food insecure, and prisoners. This is all also profoundly scriptural (see e.g., Rom 16:7, Jas 1:27, 1 Tim 6:8).

We pray for the United States and all who are in authority:

> Our Father in heaven, your kingdom come; and may the President, all leaders of this nation, and the leaders of the world know that your Son, Jesus Christ, the king of the world is coming again. May they seek justice for the poor, and love their neighbors. Holy Spirit, draw them to the Father.

The reason we pray for leaders is because the Scriptures tell us we must: 1 Timothy 2:1–2 tells us to pray for "kings and all who are in high positions." We anticipate the first line of the Lord's Prayer with the first line to remind ourselves that, as the church, we don't seek the kingdoms of this world. We seek rather the new heavens and the new earth. Praying that the POTUS and every national leader at home or abroad would remember that Jesus is the true King is the most loving thing we can pray for them. It is for their good that they exercise their authority knowing they will be judged before God's throne. This is also why we pray the Spirit would draw them to the Father. By praying that they would remember the poor and love their neighbors, we remind ourselves what standard the Scriptures hold rulers to. The love command is obvious. But we also mention specifically the poor because, if Mary's Magnificat offers any hope for the rich and the powerful, it is through the care and regard for the poor that they can anticipate the coming judgment (Luke 1:52–53).

Finally, we pray for the welfare of the world again in trinitarian fashion:

> Father, give this world its daily bread. We pray for those who hunger and thirst: Jesus, give them your righteousness. Holy Spirit, we pray against war, strife, death and destruction of all forms. Bring your peace to this world. (Prayer for particular countries happens here).

The anticipatory reference to the Lord's prayer reminds us that God is the one who feeds the world. The next sentence combines the spiritual and the physical into one prayer. Those who hunger and thirst physically ought not only to trust God for their daily bread, but must also seek his righteousness. This is based in the Beatitudes: "Blessed are those who hunger and thirst for righteousness, for they shall be filled" (Matt 5:6). Finally, we pray eschatologically—again in keeping with the ethos of the Lord's Prayer. All wars will cease when the Spirit ushers in the peace of God's kingdom.

We conclude the time of prayer with praying the Lord's Prayer itself corporately. This both sums up everything else we have prayed and ensures that nothing is missed in how Christ has invited us to pray.

Prayer in and from Every Tongue

As I said in the introduction, Resurrection Assembly is a diverse church. We have people from numerous languages, every class, and all age groups. Given that the Scriptures speak of every tongue confessing and every knee bowing to Jesus on the Last Day (Phil 2:10–11), and given that Jesus himself told his disciples to let the children come to him (Mark 10:14), we have felt compelled to invite (and indeed insist) that everyone present be allowed to participate in the performance of our liturgy.

Our "everyone participates" attitude is founded, like everything else I have detailed in this chapter, on trinitarian worship. We take a strong stance that to truly participate in God's trinitarian life, one needs to be baptized. Yet, we equally claim that God as Trinity is our all-encompassing reality. It is the reality even those who do not worship God as Trinity inhabit. As Paul himself declared to the pagan philosophers at the Areopagus, the trinitarian God is the one in whom "we live and move and are" (Acts 17:28). Everyone who steps through the doors of the church lives and moves and has their being in God. Why can't they begin to recognize and engage that by participating in worship of their Creator?

Our conviction that anyone and everyone can participate in the liturgy stands in stark contrast to the consumer-oriented church growth models of evangelism. We do not believe that people should sit back, watch a show-like presentation of the gospel, and then either accept or reject the proposition that "Jesus is Lord." Of course we want people ultimately to accept or reject Jesus, but we believe that the moment of decision might escape a time stamp. We believe a person participates in worship, and then can find at some point down the road of worship that they have been formed into an entirely different person.

Still, what does this "everyone-participates" commitment look like concretely? We have children lead the Lord's Prayer, the Apostles' Creed, and the Mystery of Faith ("Christ has died; Christ is Risen; Christ will come again"). Normally, we have mature Christians lead public prayer (this is exclusively the case for altar prayer leaders, for obvious reasons), but no one is excluded who wants to make petitions to God. Everyone who leads public prayer is invited to pray in their mother tongue. We regularly have prayed in French, Spanish, and Swahili, among others. We pray the Lord's Prayer in whatever language is present that given Sunday.

We also wait until right before the liturgy begins to select Scripture readers and communion servers. That way we can make sure to invite different people from week to week to participate. Waiting until the final moment does create some hiccups in the movements of the liturgy. Some people fiddle with the microphone trying to unmute it. Sometimes people forget it's their turn to read a Scripture. This creates some long moments of silence, and sometimes necessitates giving people prompts in the midst of our worship. But that is no matter. We are not putting on a show. We are worshipping God: Father, Son, and Holy Spirit.

. . .

Our baptismal font is a horse trough. We bought it at a local farm supply store. We store it in the church shed outside, so every baptism requires preparation days ahead of time. We retrieve the trough from the shed several days before we plan on baptizing to clean it, and to check it for leaks. Sometimes we need to caulk the seams of the tank and leave it to dry in the sun. We then lay out plastic tarps in front of the altar so as not to soak the carpet, and as a secondary precaution for smaller leaks that may have gone undetected. We fill up the tank the night before with hose water. Even in the summer, Iowan hose water is frigid—and it's even more so in the winter. So we submerge water heaters that we also bought at the farm supply store which are normally used to keep the drinking water in liquid form for livestock. When we baptize, the whole church leaves their seats to gather at the altar and stand around the trough. When the baptisand emerges from the water, there is a shout, a round of applause, and smiles all around—heralding the split in the sky and the quickening of resurrection.

After baptisms, there's an almost equal amount of work to do. The water needs to be pumped out of the tank, tarps need to be folded and stored, and the tank needs to be carried out by a couple of people with sufficient upper body strength.

From an outsider's perspective, this may seem like tremendous effort for what turns out to be such an unglamorous event. It takes days of preparation for the few moments it takes to say, "I baptize you in the name of the Father, Son, and Holy Spirit." But this is the work of the church. And putting in all of the effort that we do through sponsorships, baptismal classes, the liturgy, the trough set up not only involves the whole church, it also reminds the church who we are. The sight of the bright blue tarps and a dull grey horse trough puts a thrill in our hearts because we know that the water in that trough isn't just Iowa City city utility water. It is the Jordan River. It is the Red Sea. It is the Noah's flood. It is death, and it is newness of life.

Questions for Reflection and Discussion

1. In your estimation, what does the average congregant at your church think is their primary and formative identity? What other identities, loyalties, and allegiances compete with their Christianity?

2. Does your church have an understanding of itself as the temple of the Holy Spirit? What are some ways you can cultivate a shared baptismal identity?

3. How does your church remind people of the basic story and confession of Christianity on a weekly basis? Does it happen in any way outside of the sermon?

4. Do you pray corporately every Sunday? Do you pray extemporaneously? Or do you prepare words ahead of time? Do you pray in a trinitarian fashion? Give reasons for your answers, and consider what might change.

Eucharistic Worship

Sermons at Resurrection Assembly always conclude with an invitation to pray a prayer of repentance. We do this because we are about to approach the Lord's Table. We specifically say that we are confessing our sins to God and to each other. That's because the communion we are about to have at the Table is communion not only with God, but also with the church. Once we have confessed our sins, I remind the church that the Scriptures promise us that since we have confessed our sins, God is faithful and just to forgive us (1 John 1:9). We then come to the altar.

The church's worship ought always to be eucharistic. I mean that in two, related ways. First, the church's worship must always be an act of thanksgiving, which is what the Greek root for "eucharist" means. The Psalms are replete with the command to "give thanks" (see e.g., Ps 33:2, 100:4). The earliest church in the book of Acts is said to have eaten "with glad and generous hearts, praising God" (Acts 2:46). Thanksgiving and praise befits the people of God. The second and related way that the church's worship must always be eucharistic is by celebrating the Eucharist, the Lord's Supper. Without the Eucharist, the church is hard-pressed to claim they are actually giving thanks appropriately for Jesus's sacrifice, which the Scriptures explicitly say was "for us" (Eph 5:2).

We celebrate and give thanks by observing the Lord's Supper every Sunday service and at most other church gatherings, abstaining only when we gather at a location or a time that not everyone in the church can access. We began celebrating the Lord's Supper every Sunday within a few months of my pastoral ministry, making it one of the first major changes we made to Sunday morning services. One leader at Resurrection feared that the Lord's Supper might actually become less special if we celebrated it all the time. I have heard this concern echoed by leadership in other churches. This has not been our experience. But even if our experience was otherwise, we are still compelled to celebrate the Supper. The most basic reason we do is because Jesus commanded his church, "do this!" (Luke 22:19). So we do.

I will explain why we celebrate the Lord's Supper with such regularity by first considering the example set forth in the Scriptures. Scripture models elaborate and elaborately deliberate worship. From there, I will rehearse the communion liturgy we follow, connecting it to trinitarian worship. And finally, I will show how the Lord's Supper informs other aspects of our church's worship and life together.

Elaborate Worship

God told Moses to construct the tabernacle according to the pattern that he would show him on the mountain (Exod 25:9). He showed him not only the tabernacle, but also the tabernacle implements. God instructed Moses and the people how to build the ark of the covenant down to the most obscure details—its dimensions, type of wood to use, and the craftsmen's method. The cherubim were to be "hammered" (Exod 25:18). The curtains were to be made of goat's hair (Exod 26:7). Solomon's temple was built with an equal attention to detail. Proportions were laid out precisely. In 2 Chronicles 4, we get details about the temple's furnishings, down to the number and style of lamp stands and basins for washing.

Israel's attention to detail in the construction of tabernacle and temple was met with an equal attention to the details of proper worship. Priests were to be consecrated through the sacrifice of a bull and two unblemished rams (Lev 8:2). Unleavened bread along with cakes, oil, and wafers were all to be present. The priests were to be washed at the tent of meeting before Aaron was to put on his priestly ephod, a sort of ceremonial tunic (Exod 29:1–9). On this ephod twelve stones with the names of the twelves tribes were installed, pointing to the high priest's role as mediator between God and his people (Exod 28:21). Leviticus goes on to describe in incredible detail the proper sacrifices that Israelites could make. The details concern not only that the animals should be without blemish, but also matters such as, in the case of a burnt offering from the flock, the offering was supposed to be killed on the north side of the altar (Lev 1:11). The building, the curtains, the clothes, the food: everything was precisely detailed. Israel's worship was elaborate and elaborately deliberate.

We see similar attention to detail in worship in the book of Revelation. Of course, here it is not a list of commands about how to build a sanctuary or how to worship properly. John merely describes what he sees when he is taken into the heavenly throne room—which is the heavenly temple—by the Spirit (Rev 4:1–2). Like the tabernacle and temple of ancient Israel, John sees precious jewels adorning God's presence. Before the throne, there is a sea of glass that clearly recalls the sea of cast metal before the altar in Solomon's temple (Rev 4:6; cf. 2 Chr 4:1–2).

The detail of the heavenly temple's adornments is matched by an equal attention to the pattern of worship in heaven. Twenty-four elders are seated on thrones and four living creatures—representatives of all of creation—are all around the throne upon which God sits. John says that all day and all night they never cease to worship. Not only that, they repeat the same words over and over again: "Holy, holy, holy, is the Lord God Almighty, who was and is and is coming!" In an elaborate performance, the elders fall down before the throne, casting down their crowns, and say, "Worthy are you our Lord and God to receive glory and honor and power" (Rev 4:6–11). There is a pattern of proper worship in heaven. It is elaborate and elaborately deliberate. It is a heavenly liturgy.

. . .

The contemporary church finds itself suspended between ancient Israel's and John's eschatological liturgies. As I said in the Introduction, if you walk into an average evangelical or Pentecostal church in the West, you will find a liturgy. But, it is generally unarticulated and, in many instances, intentionally uninvolved and uncomplicated. These simplified liturgies of four to five songs, offering, sermon, and dismissal do not find their history in ancient Israel, and they don't find their fulfillment in John's eschatological visions. It's my contention (and the practice of Resurrection Assembly) that the church's liturgy ought to find itself firmly in that context. Indeed, it is the only way to have biblical worship.

Now, there are of course exceptions to the rule of your average evangelical church. There are historic Protestant churches that might call themselves evangelical who have liturgies that are highly intentional and biblically informed. Many of these liturgies find their roots in the Catholic and Orthodox church's attempts to situate the church's worship between Israel and Revelation as I have detailed. With that in mind, the worry that some of my fellow evangelical and Pentecostal readers might have is that such elaborate liturgies ultimately fail to teach an "authentic" faith. Questions will be asked: "Might individual churchgoers never make the Faith their own by relying too much on overly formalized patterns of worship?" And, "is such elaborate liturgy not the major cause of the widespread dilution of the Christian faith into cultural symbols across western Europe?"

Such concerns seem to me to be contrived and ultimately misguided. By what analysis can anyone prove that liturgy was instrumental in any given historic church's decline? Does the repetitive heavenly worship modeled in Revelation 4 produce a lackadaisical attitude about holy things amongst the twenty-four elders? Again, the question here—ultimately—is, "What is biblical?" That's not the same thing as asking, "What is effective?" There is no guarantee that biblical worship will always see the church grow and multiply and mature according to our best wishes. Many walked away from Jesus when he invited them to come die with him. Even his own disciples betrayed the shallowness of their faith when they abandoned him on the night of his arrest.

The task of the church is to be biblically faithful—that's it. Biblical faithfulness is no simple task given the wide and varied witness of the Scriptures, and the wide and varied interpretations of the Scriptures throughout Christian history. But it seems to me to be an obvious error to avoid this tremendous task in the name of being practical. I do not deny that the historic liturgical churches have failed to be faithful in some respects. Who hasn't? And I am not proposing that Pentecostals become Anglicans! Whatever the failures of historic churches, they must be held up to the standards of the Scriptures. Our task remains simply to be faithful interpreters of the Scriptures in our context. To be faithful to the Scripture's account of elaborate worship is not to mimic others, or to embrace hallow ritual, but to be more truly who God has called us, his church, to be.

Evangelicalism in the United States itself does not escape the critique of reducing the Christian faith to culture. How many adherents are in my own fellowship, the Assemblies of God, because of cultural reasons, not kingdom ones? Only God knows hearts, but we should judge not the historic church lest we ourselves be judged.

This brings me to another—and in my opinion, problematic—exception to the rule of unreflective and emaciated liturgies. Consider the elaborate liturgies of church-growth modeled megachurches and megachurch-hopefuls. Below the simple surface, the liturgy is in fact elaborate. Songs are sung with impeccable musicianship. The stage lights pan out on the crowd just as the chorus hits. The strobe flashes at the bridge. There are screens facing the stage (note: It's rarely called an "altar") so the worship team can see the countdown timer until the pastor appears to facilitate a "transition" to the next movement of the service. Fog machines pump out an atmosphere. But what is that atmosphere? Never has a church with fog machines rationalized their use by appealing to ancient Israel's burning of incense in the temple. Nor do they appeal to the angel's procession with the censor of incense in the heavenly throne room when the seventh seal is broken by the Lamb in the book of Revelation (Rev 8:1–5). No—the logic seems more to come from the liturgies established by pop concerts and the Super Bowl. Indeed, I have been in churches that are indistinguishable from a nightclub except that the alcohol has been replaced with coffee and sexualized dancing has been replaced with the glamor of the perfectly tailored outfits on stage (again, not an "altar").

Is there something wrong with fog machines? Not intrinsically. But if there is no biblical reason for why we do what we do in worship, then it's all just gimmicks. Our liturgies should confront the nightclub and Super Bowl liturgies of this world with the kingdom God. There is nothing wrong with having fun and being entertained. But that form of church is not only unsatisfying from a Christian perspective, but would also seem, in the long run, to beget the very nominalism "authentic" evangelicalism wants to avoid.

At Resurrection Assembly, we wanted the new covenant that Jesus established at the Last Supper and achieved in his death, resurrection, and ascension to be the foundation of our liturgy and our church life together. We wanted this for the biblical reasons I stated in the introduction. Jesus said "do this!" So we do. Every other part of the service finds its heartbeat in that. Whatever instruments are used and songs are sung; how we collect the offering, how we invite the congregation to greet one another in the midst of the service, whatever is said from the pulpit—all of it finds its source in the communion liturgy. Communion informs what we do even before the church gathers, and after we disperse. This is seen not least in the meals—free communal breakfast and lunch—that so often bracket our Sunday morning services. But before I say a bit about communion's influence on the church's life outside of our Sunday morning service, let me explain how we celebrate our communion liturgy and what exactly we pray.

Communion: How We Celebrate

Before I narrate in specific detail the actual communion liturgy, it is really important to make explicit certain aspects of the liturgy that might otherwise go unnoticed. To begin with, we say words. Specifically, we say words that narrate the event of Jesus's death and the Last Supper. This is important to note because I have been in a number of churches and Christian gatherings that prefer not to say anything at all at what—presumably—they consider to be the Lord's Supper. I attended a church that seemingly at random would distribute a cup of grape juice and a morsel of bread in total silence. There was no declaration that it was in fact the Lord's Supper. No liturgy, no prayer, no comment. But we must say words. Baptism is not baptism unless the baptizer says, "I baptize you in the name of the Father, and of the Son, and of the Holy Spirit." Without those words, baptism is just splashing in water. Similarly, without words, the cup and the bread are merely an in-service snack that can't feed the body let alone the soul.

Another important aspect of the liturgy is that it is a prayer. The communion liturgy we use begins by addressing our "holy and gracious Father." To state the obvious, this is an acknowledgement that God is in fact present and must therefore be addressed. But more importantly, the liturgy is a prayer precisely because it is God who makes the Lord's Supper what it is. This is not witchcraft whereby our words have power in and of themselves. They are words addressed to the Father about the Son in the power of the Holy Spirit that are consistent with the Scriptures. God is in charge, not us.

The placement of the communion in the liturgy of the service is also intentional. We always wait until the culmination of the service, after the Scriptures have been preached, to celebrate and give thanks. This is not absolutely necessary, but it is fitting. Jesus's own life culminated with the institution of his new covenant. We wanted our liturgy to follow the movements of Jesus's life.

Finally, we always have a pastor lead communion. There is a certain responsibility that comes with celebrating the supper that should be on a pastor's shoulders. We don't take the stance that there is something preventing a non-clergy member from celebrating the Supper, just as there is nothing preventing a layperson from preaching. But it is not the norm and the pastoral responsibilities that come with preaching and celebrating the Supper ought to fall first and foremost on a pastor's shoulders. Paul asks the church in 1 Corinthians 11 to discern the body (1 Cor 11:29). One of Paul's main concerns is that the rich are excluding the poor (1 Cor 11:17–22). Preventing this from happening in the contemporary church often falls by default of administration to pastors, which is why it is fitting for them to lead the celebration.

We recommend people abstain from the meal unless they have been baptized. This has upset some people, and I have had people barge right up to the communion table once the service has concluded to interrogate me about this. Mind you, I have never actually "fenced the table" by forbidding someone from participating. We have only recommended that people abstain. One of the reasons I am suspicious this upsets people is that it has something to do with our consumerist culture. People are used to having the buying power to have what they want to have. And when someone tells them, "You can't have this," (especially in America) they feel this is somehow an infringement on their human right to freedom. But regardless of what the reason is, our response has always been the same: "Why are you so desperate to participate in the Lord's Supper, but not so desperate to be baptized?" Almost all of the people I have baptized at Resurrection Assembly have been prompted to baptism by this part of our communion liturgy. This highlights, again, why we reserve the celebration of the Lord's Supper for pastors. When people are offended, their offense should fall on the pastor since pastors are tasked in the first instance with shepherding God's people.

Communion: What We Pray

As I did with the corporate prayers of the previous chapter, here I detail the specific words we say. I will accompany the different sections with minimal explanation to facilitate understanding. Readers familiar with the Anglican church's Book of Common Prayer will recognize that the liturgy we use is based on the communion liturgy contained in it. We do not have profound reasons for sourcing the liturgy from the Book of Common Prayer. We use it merely because it is accessible, biblical, and the words therefore resonate across denominational lines. The proof is in the pudding.

Our communion liturgy always begins with a confession of sin:

> Because we can boldly approach the throne of grace and receive mercy, let's confess our sins to God and one another.

The Lord's Supper is Jesus's new covenant for the forgiveness of sins, which is why it is fitting to confess sins before approaching the Table. We say that we are confessing our sins to God and to one another in keeping with James 5:16, which commands the church to confess sins to one another, not only to God. A particular joy of mine has been to hear of congregants confessing to one another outside of the context of the liturgy. This is yet more evidence of the importance of intentional liturgy: it forms the day-to-day lives of participants.

After we pray a prayer of repentance I quote 1 John 1:9, and affirm God's forgiveness:

> If we confess our sins, he is faithful and just to forgive us our sins and to cleanse us from all unrighteousness.
> We have confessed our sins. God forgives us.

I then offer an invitation to Christianity and some cautionary words:

> If you are not a Christian, I urge you today to believe in the Lord Jesus Christ and be baptized that you might join us at this table. If you have not done so, I recommend you refrain from this meal for your own sake.

I invite the congregation to pray with me, and we pray the following. We put these words on the projector screen or on a bulletin so people can actually pray the words along with me. This is our commitment that the church prays for God to make the meal for us the Lord's Supper. While we say the pastor ought by default to lead the liturgy, it is in fact the whole church who prays together:

> Holy and gracious Father: In your infinite love you made us for yourself; and when we had fallen into sin and become subject to sin and death, you, in your mercy, sent Jesus Christ, your only and eternal Son, to share our human nature, to live and die as one of us, to reconcile us to you, the God and Father of all.
>
> He stretched out his arms upon the cross, and offered himself in obedience to your will, a perfect sacrifice for the whole world.
>
> On the night he was handed over to suffering and death, our Lord Jesus Christ took bread; and when he had given thanks, he broke it, and gave it to his disciples, and said, "Take, eat: This is my Body, which is given for you. Do this for the remembrance of me."
>
> After supper he took the cup of wine; and when he had given thanks, he gave it to them, and said, "Drink this, all of you: This is my Blood of the new Covenant, which is shed for you and for many for the forgiveness of sins. Whenever you drink it, do this for the remembrance of me.

The opening of the prayer offers a parallel summary to the Nicene Creed by giving a snapshot of God's work of salvation throughout the whole biblical witness, beginning with creation and the fall. The declarations that Christ is God's eternal Son who took on human nature find their source in the christological hymns of Philippians 2:6–8 and Colossians 1:15–20. Christians will recognize that the prayer from there on is based squarely on the stories of the Last Supper in the synoptic Gospels and on Paul's account in 1 Corinthians 11:23–26.

We then pray:

> We now celebrate the memorial of our redemption, O Father, in this sacrifice of praise and thanksgiving. Recalling his death, resurrection, and ascension, we offer you these gifts.
>
> Father, we ask you to sanctify these by your Holy Spirit to be for your people the Body and Blood of your Son, the food and drink of new and unending life in him.

We ask you to make us holy that we may faithfully
receive this meal, and serve you in unity, faith, and peace;
And at the last day bring us with all your church into the
joy of your eternal kingdom.

We ask all of this through your Son Jesus Christ. By
him, and with him, and in him, in the unity of the Holy
Spirit all honor and glory is yours, Almighty Father, now
and forever.

The congregation says in unison, "Amen."

An entire volume could be written on the precision of these
words and their overlap with and diversions from other historic
communion liturgies. But I will highlight only a few things.

Jesus himself told us to "do this in remembrance," so we explicitly declare—and thus remember—Jesus's death, resurrection,
and ascension. Because Jesus ascended, the Holy Spirit descended.
As such, every celebration of the Lord's Supper is like a mini-
Pentecost. Like the disciples in the upper room, we ask the Father
to send the Holy Spirit to set us on fire with his presence. As it was
for the disciples on the road to Emmaus, we believe God makes his
presence known in the breaking of bread (Luke 24:31).

Some evangelical churches and my fellow Pentecostals might
take pause at praying that God would sanctify the meal by the Holy
Spirit "to be" the body and blood of Jesus. Words like these might
worry some that it presumes a trans- or consubstantial understanding of the Lord's Supper. Without getting into these historic
debates, let me say simply that we are, as always, merely following
the words of Scripture. Jesus used the state of being verb "is" when
he said "this is my body" and "this is my blood." We therefore stick
with the state of being verb in our prayer. If Jesus says it "is" his
body and blood, then we pray that it would "be" accordingly.

Finally, we pray for unity, faith, and peace, and that God
would bring us into his eternal kingdom. All of this is scriptural.
To the matter of unity, Paul says in 1 Corinthians 10:17, "Because
there is one bread, we who are many are one body." And, in the
same context, he says that the celebration of the Lord's Supper sets
the church's eyes on the eschatological horizon: "As often as you eat

this bread and drink the cup, you proclaim the Lord's death until he comes" (1 Cor 11:26).

I then announce in accordance with 1 Corinthians 5:7–8, "Christ our Passover is sacrificed for us, we will keep the feast." We feast together with song and then we close in prayer:

> Almighty God, thank you for feeding us with the spiritual food of the Body and Blood of your Son our Savior Jesus Christ. And now, Father, send us out to do the work you have given us to do. To Jesus Christ, to you, and to the Holy Spirit, be honor and glory, now and for ever.

And the congregation once again says, "Amen."

Eucharistic Life

As I have already said, the celebration of the Lord's Supper does not strictly begin with the liturgy we pray. Nor does it end with the concluding doxology. Our goal as a church that needed to be revitalized was to have the Eucharist inform how we did and continue to do life together. We wanted to live a eucharistic life.

Again, the Scriptures here set the example. On the road to Emmaus, the two disciples were kept from recognizing their risen Lord until he broke bread with them (Luke 24:30–31). The moment was not necessarily the Eucharist itself, but it was eucharistic. Similarly, when the crew on the ship carrying the prisoner Paul had lost all hope in the darkness of the storm at sea, Paul took bread, gave thanks, and broke it—just as Jesus had done at the Last Supper— and gave it to the famished sailors (Acts 27:33–36). It wasn't done explicitly in remembrance of Jesus, but the meal is clearly modeled on how Jesus himself handed the bread out to the five thousand, the disciples at the Last Supper, and those on the road to Emmaus.

Our goal was to make other habits in our church similarly recall and find their source in the celebration of the meal Jesus commanded us to observe. This began with sharing meals together, and ended with all things common.

When I became the lead pastor of the church in January 2016, the one ministry that was still full of life in the church was the Sunday and Wednesday night kids and teens ministry. A good majority of the kids came without parents, kids who would be reduced to the stereotype of "at-risk" by the public school system.[1] Kids came hungry, both for a meal to fill their empty stomachs and for every word that comes from the mouth of God. So we gave them both. Pastor Abby Anderson and her husband Kyle—who was the youth pastor at the time—were providing breakfast and lunch to the kids on either side of the Sunday morning worship service and an evening meal on Wednesdays after kid and youth-oriented worship.

I knew that this ministry was vital to the church. After all, Jesus did tell his disciples to let the children come to him (Mark 10:13–16). But there were problems. Not with the kids or the Andersons, but with the whole church's perception of this profound ministry. The problem was seen most clearly in the fact that the kids and youth had been all but banished from the main sanctuary and its regular worship. Kids would come to church and be sent downstairs to worship apart from the adults. The children were permitted to re-emerge only after the adults had left. At best, there was a general indifference amongst the leadership toward the children. At worst, they had contempt for them. One leader went as far to complain that the church's job was not to run a "ghetto babysitting service." Clearly, he was not only anti-child, but also was not a little bit racist.

There is a sense in which I agreed with this former leader—minus, of course, the racist bit. He and I agreed that the church's mission is not to be just another nonprofit giving handouts to those we otherwise feel indifferent to. We are called, child and

---

1. Pastor Abby Anderson always notes the implicit condescension and dehumanization of labels like "at-risk." They are necessary at times so public schools can describe their populations for grant-writing purposes. But, in our view, any child or teen we have had the privilege of enjoying a meal with is just as much "at-risk" of being filled with the Holy Spirit to prophesy and dream dreams as anything else.

adult alike, to share at a common table in the fellowship of the Holy Spirit. This leader could not see the solution because he had the mistaken premise that children can't participate fully in the church. There is of course nothing wrong with being a soup kitchen. But the church's mission is much more than that. We are to feed people with every word that comes from the mouth of God, which, as I already have said, just happened to be the very thing the kids were hungry for. It was also the very thing we were eager to do.

So, again, the solution for this problem was to have the kids share at the same table as the adults. And in order to do that, we needed to have a common table at which to eat. The Lord's Supper thus became the central symbol of our church's revitalization.

With the regular observance of the Lord's Supper, we were able to connect what was happening in the Eucharist with our church life together. Though the meals we shared on Wednesday nights and on Sundays predated the implementation of the Eucharist into our Sunday morning liturgy, all of the sudden they made sense only in light of it. Jesus himself invites us to feast on his body and blood every week. How could we not show the same generosity and hospitality in the meals we shared from our church kitchen? The thanks we gave for the meals we shared as a community made sense in light of the thanks were giving every Sunday morning at the Eucharist. For those who didn't see the connection with their own eyes, we explained it from the pulpit.

. . .

From there, our practice of eucharistic generosity and hospitality extended into the home. Pastor Abby and I hosted and continue to host people in our homes weekly. We feed them and, in doing so, thank the God who gives us our daily bread.

The church's food pantry, always open to the public, has also allowed us to take this eucharistic spirit into others' homes. Throughout the week, we visit people where they live. This is very much contrary to our contemporary American culture. People generally don't expect friends to come knocking on the door uninvited. But Pastor Abby and I do it anyway. It reminds our congregants that Jesus is always standing at the door and knocking, and he always has five loaves of bread and two fish in his hands.

One of the most obvious, yet consistently overlooked and unstated facts about the Lord's Supper is that it never runs out. Wherever there is bread and even just a drop of wine, we can give thanks and celebrate. If there is an earthly famine, and therefore no bread or wine, the Lord's Supper still does not run out, because Jesus's body and blood, resurrected and exalted to the right hand of the Father, is eternal. We have extended this eucharistic conviction—that there is always enough and that there is always more—and applied it to the life of the church.

The food pantry is again an instructive example. No matter how much food we have handed out, and no matter how many times it looked like we might run out, it never has. No one who has wanted food has gone without when they have come to Resurrection Assembly. Indeed, there have been times where we have mistakenly tried to ration fresh produce. But almost without fail it rots the moment we try to save some for another day. Like manna, it appears day after day when we need it to feed the hungry—as long as we are faithful to distribute it. And like the twelve apostles, we seem always to find there are baskets and baskets left over even when we've done everything to feed every hungry mouth.

The book of Acts gives us a picture of the earliest church as those who had "all things common" (Acts 2:44; 4:32). Central to having all things common was the sharing of bread in each others' homes (Acts 2:42). But it went well beyond that to the selling of property and the laying of the proceeds at the apostles' feet for distribution to those in need (Acts 4:34–35). In other words, their eucharistic life together went well beyond the sharing of bread. But the sharing of bread was at the same time the first movement, the foundational reason they could have all things common.

At Resurrection Assembly, we sought to follow the example set for us in the Scriptures. We still very much trust the Spirit to teach us how to do this more fully and more joyfully. But we see signs that we are beginning to hold all things common. People share of their time and their energy. They consider each others' problems their own problems. If someone can't pay rent, everyone knows and cares, and does what they can to help. We rejoice together when one of us gets a new job. We cry together when one of us faces eviction. As the kids at Resurrection Assembly always say, "We eat the bread and drink the cup: We are one."

The unity we have at Resurrection is evidence of our revitalization, and our revitalization is evidence of our resurrecting worship. Clearly, the unity we have was not always present, and we must continually seek it by the power of the Spirit, even as the church in Acts had to. The liturgy of this chapter is all about cultivating the eucharistic life. I have spoken of the communion table, the pantry, sharing meals together, and the common life. It is fitting to close with one final example of our eucharistic liturgy and life.

Two Penny Offering

We decided that if we were to learn to have all things common as a church, then we would need to practice all of us giving. The offering is where this takes place. As I have said, many people at Resurrection have very little, and some have nothing at all. The children in particular don't have many possessions—if any—to give, especially not money. So we implemented what we call our "two-penny offering."

I introduce the offering by reminding people of the widow Jesus pointed out in the temple (Luke 21:1–4). She gave two pennies and he said that she gave more than everyone else did because while others gave out of their abundance, she gave out of her poverty. I then invite the congregation to give out of their poverty. At that moment, an usher walks the central aisle with a plate of pennies. Everyone, rich or poor, is invited to step out of their seat, take two pennies and put them, with whatever other offering they have, in the offering plate. The offering plate sits on the same altar at which we will celebrate the Lord's Supper minutes later.

I have often remarked that the kids in our church have always been our biggest and most generous givers. Every week, someone gives the penniless children two pennies. And every week they give all they have. To the world's eye, it may look like a gimmick that merely gives the appearance of adolescent participation. But like a cup of grape juice and a small cracker is said to "be" Jesus's body and blood, when offered in faith, two pennies might just be all the money in the world.

Questions for Reflection and Discussion

1. Do you celebrate the Lord's Supper every week? Why or why not?

2. How does/ought the Lord's Supper inform the life of your church?

3. What requirements do you place on individuals for participating in the Lord's Supper?

4. How does your church's offering practices give witness to the Bible's call to have all things common?

Pentecostal Worship

Omari Kabwe prays in another tongue. He is from the Kivu region of the Democratic Republic of Congo. He and his family fled the ongoing conflict, ending up at a refugee camp in Malawi. From there, he came to the United States through Germany, landing first in Arizona before coming to Iowa City. He and his family, including six children, are now US citizens. When there is any matter big or small, the whole church knows that Omari will pray about it—if indeed he knows about. Recognizing his spiritual gifting, we have made a habit of having him lead prayer in our Sunday liturgy. He always blesses the church in English, but when he begins to pray, he switches to his first language, Swahili. At Resurrection, we celebrate the spiritual giftings of every member of the body of Christ. We pray in other tongues, we celebrate words of encouragement in testimony, individuals sing a capella spiritual solos, and acts of service are done in secret.

We are a Pentecostal church. That identity has in many circles come to signify a certain charismatic expression in word and song. Speaking in another tongue—whether a human or a heavenly one—is taken to be integral to this charismatic expression. Still, our Pentecostal liturgy is much deeper than enthusiastic outbursts in this or that language. We of course regularly have people who shout out praise to God. We also have a lot of verbal interplay between the altar and the congregation—an extemporaneous, but no less established, liturgy of "amens" shouted when a person feels a moment needs particular and public affirmation. Sometimes I will provoke an "amen" by asking for it in the midst of the sermon.

As I said in the introduction of this book, to be Pentecostal is to live out the events at the beginning of the book of Acts. Jesus instituted a new covenant in his body and blood. He died and rose again. He ascended to the right hand of the Father, and poured out the Holy Spirit on the church. A wind brought the fire of God on them, and they—like Omari—spoke in other tongues. All of this meant one thing, according to the book of Acts. Peter got up on the day of Pentecost and said, "these are the last days" (Acts 2:17).

The biblical story's order of the Lord's Supper, death, resurrection, and ascension, culminating in Pentecost demonstrates the unity of worship that this book is all about. Pentecost represents the trinitarian fulfillment of eucharistic worship. In other words, trinitarian and eucharistic worship must result in Pentecostal worship. And to be Pentecostal means to live in the last days by the power of the Holy Spirit.

This chapter is about the Pentecostal ethos of our liturgy. Of course, the last two chapters are themselves an exposition of our Pentecostal worship, since to be Pentecostal is necessarily to be trinitarian and eucharistic, but here I highlight the characteristics of our worship that might be uniquely identified as "Pentecostal." End-times preaching is at the center. With that, the public reading of Scripture, song, and "altar calls"—a time of consecration in prayer—are important and indispensable corollaries. Scripture, song, preaching, and altar calls are all important in their own right. But these spiritual acts of worship also address the worldly realities the congregants of Resurrection face. I conclude this chapter with a couple of testimonies about how the end times confronts our suffering.

Scripture

On the day of Pentecost, Peter prophesies in the power of the Holy Spirit. Pentecostals expect to do the same. The outpouring of the Holy Spirit on the church means that is possible. Peter not only demonstrates that the Spirit empowers for prophecy, but also shows the form prophecy should take. He stands up and announces that the last days have arrived (Acts 2:17). To support this claim, he recounts the recent event of Jesus's resurrection, and correlates that event with the Scriptures. At Resurrection Assembly, we were convinced that if we wanted to live out Pentecost as the earliest church did, and so worship as those who anticipate resurrection, we needed to follow Peter's pattern. Our Pentecostal liturgy needs to start with the proclamation of the Scriptures, so that we, too, might prophesy by the power of the Holy Spirit.

The Scriptures function for us in two complimentary and mutually informing ways. First, they help us understand contemporary events—political, sociological, environmental, and so on. They also help us appraise our ongoing tribulations and joys. Secondly—and this is indispensable—the Scriptures help us see what story we are living. The Scriptures narrate one big story, from creation to the virgin birth to a city called the new Jerusalem coming down out of heaven. Some of that story is past, some of it is present, and some of it is yet to come. All of it, however, is our story. And we are living it out by the power of the Spirit.

This is exactly how the Scriptures functioned for Peter on the day of Pentecost.

First, he uses the Scriptures to appraise contemporary events. The Spirit was poured out with a wind and with tongues of fire, so he quotes Joel 2:28–32 to explain it. God had promised this joy in Joel when he spoke through the prophet, "I will pour out my Spirit on all flesh" (Joel 2:28, cf. Acts 2:17). Peter does the same thing with Jesus's resurrection and ascension. The Spirit is poured out because Jesus had been raised from the dead and ascended, and this was foretold by the prophet, King David. He foretold that the Lord would say to his Lord, "sit at my right hand" (Acts 2:34, cf. Ps 109:1), and that he would say this because he would not let his "Holy One see corruption" (Acts 2:27).

But, again, the Scriptures did not just explain events in some willy-nilly prooftexting fashion for Peter. He was drawing together the story that God was telling. The God of Israel, the One who had made the heavens and the earth, had now acted in raising Jesus from the dead. Peter admits that his hearers might have thought that the words spoken about a "holy one" not seeing corruption would be about David, since they were words attributed to his mouth. Peter reasons these words could not have been about David because everyone knows David is dead and did in fact see corruption. Thus what has happened to Jesus is the continuing story the God of Israel is telling about the world. Finally, all of this means that—like any story—the end is coming. "These are the last days." Resurrection has happened, the Spirit is poured out, now is the time to be saved from "this crooked generation" (Acts 2:40). The implication is, of course, that judgment is coming, and a glorious new creation is dawning.

To be Pentecostal is to live in the pre-dawn light. It is to take the Scriptures so seriously that we appraise our daily lives with them, and it means to always place ourselves in the grand trinitarian story of the Bible. To be Pentecostal is to ask, "What time is it?" and to always respond by saying, "The night is far gone, for now salvation is nearer than when we first believed" (Rom 13:12, 11). The light of the sunrise about to visit us from on high is already peeking over the horizon. That light is the Spirit poured out.

Again, in order to be prophetic like Peter, both in appraising our daily lives and announcing the coming kingdom, we needed the Scriptures to be central to all we do. As I have said many times already, we wanted our worship to be biblical. It is not enough for things to be biblical in the sense that we use it as a reference guide. The Bible itself must be central and indispensable to the performance of our liturgy. To make it so at Resurrection Assembly, we started reading it out loud, sometimes in large portions, as an act of worship.

. . .

Every Sunday, we read at minimum three passages of Scripture out loud. Two are intertwined with song, creed, and offering leading up to the sermon. The third is read either in preparation for, or as part of the sermon itself. With the first two readings, we offer little to no commentary on the passages. The only matters we address are, for example, if the passage comes at a time when a pronoun's referent is unclear. But all of the Scripture readings correlate in terms of content, with the first two passages contributing to what the sermon will be about. Normally, the preacher for the day selects the passages, but we at times source the passages from a lectionary that follows the liturgical calendar like one might find in the Book of Common Prayer.

The Scripture passages, whether from a lectionary or chosen by the preacher, coalesce thematically. So, for example, if I am preaching about baptism, we might read one of the Gospel narrative accounts of Jesus's own baptism, one of Paul's teachings about baptism (e.g., Rom 6:1–4), and an Old Testament passage such as the crossing of the Red Sea or Noah's flood since the New Testament refers to both of those events as baptisms (see 1 Cor 10:1–2 and 1 Pet 3:20–21, respectively).

In the sermon the focus is on one passage, but we almost always make reference to the other passages to make their thematic unity explicit. We will often have at least one passage from both Testaments, that way we are always deliberate in witnessing to the whole canon of the church. There are some exceptions to this. For a time, we were preaching through the book of Revelation. Taking Revelation's lead when it says, "Blessed is the one who reads [aloud] the words of this prophecy" (Rev 1:3), each Sunday we would read consecutive passages out loud so that, at the end of the series, we had read the entire book of Revelation out loud together. (In faith, we were indeed blessed).

We have a separate pulpit, just in front of the altar, from which the Scriptures are read. The Scriptures are a part of our liturgy where anyone can participate. Even non-Christians can read a passage of Scripture should they want to do so. We always wait to select Scripture readers until right before our liturgy formally begins in order to maximize participation by including different people every week. As mentioned before, this means we have some hiccups in liturgy where people miss their cues or fiddle with the microphone, but we don't occupy ourselves with putting on a perfect show, because that's not what worship is. Even on the day of Pentecost in Acts, there was some ruckus and confusion on the part of both participants and onlookers (some suggested, "these people are drunk" Acts 2:13). As Pentecostals, we expect it to be no different in our contemporary setting.

With the first Scripture reading we always make clear why we are doing what we are doing. I already mentioned Revelation's promise of blessing for reading it out loud, but 1 Timothy 4:13 applies it to the whole of the Christian Scriptures. The verse tells the early church to devote itself to the public reading of Scripture. So we say, "Because the Bible tells us to devote ourselves to the public reading of Scripture we read from . . ." We then name the book, chapter, and verse numbers of the passage to be read. To put it plainly, if we want the Bible to be central to all that we do, we need to heed the Bible's charge to read the Scriptures out loud in church.

. . .

This biblical injunction to read the Bible is particularly important in our contemporary setting. Biblical literacy is in crisis in the church in the United States. Whether it has ever been different is a moot question. The problem simply persists that most Christians don't make a habit of reading the Scriptures either individually in the privacy of their own lives or in corporate contexts. And they don't understand what they are reading. The churches that still read the Scriptures out loud as part of their historic liturgies with a few (but significant) exceptions have jettisoned the study of the Bible as that which exists "for our instruction" (Rom 15:4). The ongoing attempts on the part of evangelical and Pentecostal churches to encourage private study, while to be applauded, will never suffice to equip the church for its God-given task in the world. The church needs to read the Scriptures out loud together so that individual Christians are not left to their own brilliance (or the terrifying feeling that they have none) to discern the one grand story that the Bible is. I have often held up a Bible at Resurrection for people to see and noted that it is a really thick book with a lot of words—and a lot of confusing words at that. Without the church's help, few individuals will ever discern what the Bible is truly about.

Furthermore, we live in a "workaholic" society. We are a society that never sleeps. In view of that, we need forms of Christian discipleship that both accommodate and confront the incredible hours people—and especially the poor—work. We need Christian discipleship for truck drivers, people who work the third shift (12 AM–8 AM) at the Whirlpool factory, and food delivery drivers. This is not to mention full-time caregivers both of children and the elderly (most of whom are the opposite of affluent). At Resurrection, we of course condemn the sabbathless society we live in and pray regularly that God would give relief to hourly wage workers. But while we wait for God to give justice to the poor, we must read the Scriptures out loud as often as we gather together as a church. It may be most peoples' only opportunity to hear the Scriptures uninterrupted and with their full attention.

I have often told the people of Resurrection Assembly that the Apostles' Creed and the Nicene Creed, both of which we regularly recite, provide a helpful summary of the whole story of the Bible. The creeds confess God: Father, Son, and Holy Spirit, and that is really, in the end, what the Bible is all about. The Bible is, in long form, the story the trinitarian God is telling about himself and his creation. This has been a helpful tool for people who try to read the Bible on their own. But even the creeds fall short of the task Christians have since the creeds say very little about the Old Testament, let alone stories of Jesus's life. In sum, reading the Scriptures out loud in church is not only to obey the Scripture's command to do so, it is also an important and necessary remedy for the many bewildered Christians who need the Bible to encourage them in their day to day lives, but don't know how to read it. Even more importantly, we believe the Scriptures can set us on Pentecostal fire.

At Resurrection, we expect every Sunday to be a road to Emmaus-like experience. The story is recorded in Luke 24, after Jesus is raised from the dead. Jesus appears to two disciples who are traveling to a town named Emmaus from Jerusalem. But their eyes are kept from recognizing him (24:16). Jesus joins them on their journey and begins to explain to them from the Scriptures how it was necessary that the Christ suffer in order to enter "into his glory" (24:26). Still not recognizing Jesus, they invite him to stay the night. At dinner he takes bread, blesses it, breaks it, and gives it to them—just as he had done for the Twelve at the Last Supper. It is in that moment they recognize Jesus, just before he vanishes. They remark afterwards that it all makes sense in retrospect: "Did not our hearts burn within us while [. . .] he opened the Scriptures to us?" (24:32).

We expect every heart to burn while the Scriptures are read and preached at Resurrection Assembly. The burning is the fire of Pentecost. After our hearts have been set on fire by the Spirit of God—the Spirit of Pentecost—we approach the Table to break bread. In that moment, we believe that we can not only recognize Jesus in our midst, but realize he has been with us from the moment we started our liturgical journey to the meal.

Singing the Scriptures

We not only read the Scriptures, we also sing them. Though it is entirely possible, and—perhaps in some instances, important—not to have music as part of a liturgy, Christian worship has almost always been musical. Music in worship is in the first instance biblical. The Israelites sang after crossing the Red Sea. Trumpets brought down the walls of Jericho. Angels sang on high of Christ's birth. The twenty-four elders in Revelation sing a new song to the Lamb who is worthy to open the scroll.

The example of Revelation is particularly illustrative of our Pentecostal worship. We sing now because we will sing on the last day. Just as we can see the dawn light before the sun has peaked over the end times horizon, so also we can hear the sound of the heavenly trumpets before we see the angelic musicians who play them. It is important, and indeed fitting, that some songs mediate suffering and tribulation (such as at funerals), but Pentecostal worship always shows preference for joy. The music we sing is supposed to be like the music of Moses, Jericho, Christ's birth, and the twenty-four elders. It is the sound of our final victory. This is, in the final instance, what resurrecting worship is about. It is about worshipping as the people who will be resurrected on the Last Day.

At Resurrection, every part of our liturgy is intertwined with song. Each song provides a refrain to Scripture, creed, offering, sermon, and Eucharist. It is another aspect of our "everyone participates" worship: the congregation ratifies and celebrates each movement of our worship with song. We begin with a call to the congregation to repeat, "blessed be God: Father, Son, and Holy Spirit." We then always invite the church to join their voices and hearts in song together. This invitation anticipates not only the unity we will experience in the Lord's Supper, but also witnesses to the incorruptible unity we will have in the new heavens and new earth.

· · ·

As I said in the chapter on trinitarian worship, we end worship with confessing and praising God as Trinity as well. We close communion by saying, "Father: to Jesus Christ, to you, and to the Holy Spirit be honor and glory now and forever." And together we sing the Doxology, a hymn of praise to Father, Son, and Holy Spirit. Music and song is the mode most appropriate to praising God and the note we end the story of our Sunday worship on, because it anticipates the Last Day when we will join our voices and our hearts with the twenty-four elders and all the heavenly host in singing praise to God.

Our aim at Resurrection Assembly is to only sing songs that are doxological—that is, songs that genuinely glorify God. A good number of songs produced by the evangelical world fall short of this standard, with lyrics that sing more about ourselves and our personal hopes and dreams than about the trinitarian God. We sing songs (however few and far between they are in the evangelical song corpus) that are rooted in the language and metaphors and stories and confessions of the Scriptures.

. . .

The musicians, and specifically the music director, at Resurrection (who happens to be my wife, Holly Lear) always work with the pastors to explore how songs might work together with the sermon and with the Scripture readings we read in the service. In this way the church can always hear the Scriptures read and preached, and then can respond with a song of approval and celebration that reflects upon what has just been read or preached. This, again, mirrors what we anticipate on the Last Day. The Lamb is announced by one of the twenty-four elders as the One worthy to open the mysterious scroll that has seven seals on it. The elders and the four living creatures fall down and worship the Lamb singing a new song in response to the Lamb taking the scroll. In a similar way, we—the church, the body of Christ who are one with the Lamb—open the scroll of the Bible week after week, and our response always is to bow down and worship in song.

Preaching

Coming back to the day of Pentecost: those in Jerusalem heard the church singing a cappella the mighty works of God (Acts 2:11), and Peter explains that this is all in fulfillment of the Scriptures. At Resurrection Assembly, we follow this example. Song and Scripture are necessary but not sufficient components for our Pentecostal worship. We need to explain the Scriptures. Preaching is central to worship, and preaching—as it was for Peter on the day of Pentecost—is always prophecy. We proclaim the mystery of the faith, that Christ has died, Christ is risen, and Christ will come again. We of course do this in the eucharistic liturgy too. But the sermon not only belabors what might be missed in the words we pray at communion, it also works out the details of what this end times message we preach means for this present moment.

. . .

Preaching should always be end times preaching, so that is what we aim to do. This is not only in keeping with our name, Resurrection Assembly, and therefore with the theme of this book. It is also profoundly biblical and Pentecostal. From the calling of Abraham where God promises him a glorious end of all nations being blessed in him to every jot and tittle of the New Testament, the Scriptures continually set the reader's eyes to the end times horizon. I have often challenged people to read the New Testament to find any part, book, or letter that doesn't frame everything with an eager anticipation of Christ's return. There are of course some who have tried to say that there is some evidence in the NT that end times fervor was already tapering off by the time the first generation of Christians were being laid to rest. But I find this is overstated, if not contrived. 2 Peter 3 explicitly addresses concerns of the delay of Christ's return and the author's response was just what astronomers with all their modern telescopic equipment say about time generally: a day is like a thousand years and a thousand years like a day in the grand scheme of God's cosmological history.

. . .

Pentecostals have been known for their end times excesses. The earliest Pentecostal movement that burgeoned from a barn on a street called Azusa in Los Angeles was made up of the poor and disenfranchised who were reading the beginning of Acts (and the prophet Joel with it) claiming that the early 1900s were in fact, finally, the last days. The outpouring of the Holy Spirit and accompanying speaking in tongues was evidence that they were reliving and carrying out the life and mission of the earliest church. This fervor all too easily gave birth to charlatans who, if not for fame and fortune, then perhaps for a sense of control in a turbulent world, began predicting the date of Christ's return by attempting to correlate the highly complex visions John saw in Revelation with contemporary events. In my own lifetime, Y2K, the end of the Mayan calendar, and the Iran nuclear deal were subjects of regular eschatological reflection.

At the same time, I have sensed a recent countercurrent to end times excesses in Pentecostal circles. The excess has been met with yet another extreme: The abandonment of all talk of Christ's return. The shift, it seems to me, has not been orchestrated. It has been more of an atrophy. And the atrophy of end times proclamation has had a correlated inverse relationship with the rise of what many call the "prosperity gospel." This anti-gospel proclaims good health and good fortune (financially or otherwise) in day-to-day life with no regard to the church's end times calling. It has no regard for this calling, but it still is, in a sense, an end times theology. Christians have always proclaimed that in the new heavens and new earth, when God is all in all, we will indeed have perfect health and fortune because we will have resurrected bodies in the presence of the One who is our Fortune. In the prosperity gospel, these promises have been collapsed into the present moment where, by some trick or formula, we can invite (or perhaps even force) God to bring these blessings into the present moment. The blessings aren't at the end of the age, they're in a heavenly bank waiting to be withdrawn.

At Resurrection Assembly, we have been wary of both these pitfalls in our weekly proclamation of the gospel. We always want to avoid calendar-correlating pretenses as if we can know the day or the hour (cf. Acts 1:7). We also want to avoid abandoning all hope of God's kingdom in order to (supposedly) live our best lives now. We want to avoid these things because one or the other will inevitably fail us. Y2K and the end of the Mayan calendar came and went. The sheer and simple fact of human weakness, suffering, and mortality will continue to insist itself on anyone claiming to live in some Holy Spirit nirvana.

Nevertheless, we were and are convinced that the only way to avoid both pitfalls, indeed the only way to be faithful to the Scriptures generally and the beginning of Acts specifically, is to always risk both extremes. To proclaim God's end times kingdom faithfully, we preach that Jesus is coming back tomorrow, and he's going to heal you of cancer today. These things must be said with such conviction that people start squirming in their seats wondering if you're about to say that this or that president of the United States or of Russia is the antichrist. The congregation needs to start fidgeting at the prospect that you might awkwardly tell the person in the wheelchair on the front row to rise, fold up their chair, and walk.

I need to emphasize that we do not intend to reconcile the future and present realities of God's kingdom. Our calling as Christians is not to decide that purple is the net result of red and blue, but to proclaim red and to proclaim blue. Neither is it to decide that five is the equidistant point between three and seven, so rather than proclaiming three and seven we can announce five. To try to reconcile and preach a synthesis of the future and present realities of God's kingdom is another pitfall. If you're preaching that the kingdom of God is already-and-not-yet, you're not actually preaching that God's kingdom is already and not-yet. Rather than serving meat and potatoes, you end up preparing potatoes with artificial meat flavoring, or meat scraps that have been pressed like a hotdog into the shape of a potato.

. . .

Our end times proclamation at Resurrection Assembly always begins with resurrection. I have begun innumerable sermons with the phrase, "Church, we believe in the resurrection of the dead and the life of the world to come." Jesus Christ is the firstborn from the dead (Col 1:18); the church will be—and is—second-born from the dead. Resurrection is what we prophesy in our preaching not only because without it Christianity is nothing, but also because it is the event that sums up the already and the not-yet proclamation of the church. Resurrection is meat, and it is potatoes.

Let us consider how the book of Acts works out the implications of Jesus's resurrection for both the church's future hope and for their daily life.

Resurrection is what Peter proclaims on the day of Pentecost. Those outside the upper room where the disciples had just received the Holy Spirit heard the disciples speaking in other tongues. Ultimately, this leads to Peter's end times proclamation: these are the last days (Acts 2:17). But the lynchpin, the event without which end times proclamation is impossible, is Jesus's resurrection from the dead. Peter offers proof: He claims that he and the disciples with him who have just been filled with the Holy Spirit are eyewitnesses of Jesus's resurrection (Acts 2:32). Peter claims to have seen the "not-yet" because the future resurrection of all God's people has happened in Jesus. If the future has happened, then the future can't be far away. Again, these are the last days.

But, like I have already said, we proclaim at Resurrection Assembly that Jesus is coming back tomorrow, but he is going to heal you today. This, too, is in the book of Acts. There are a host of ways of seeing this through, for example, Peter's and Paul's prison escapes and a shipwreck-turned-salvation. But perhaps the simplest way of showing this is through the healing of paralytics, one at the gate called Beautiful, and one named Aeneas.

Acts portrays the healing of these two miracles as resurrections. To really see this, a reader of Acts needs to make use of the imagination. In ancient times, there were no wheelchairs. If you were paralyzed and therefore unable to walk, you would have to lay on a mat or a bed. Others would carry you where you needed to go (cf. Mark 2:1–12). Paralytics, in other words, were in a death-posture. The dead, like paralytics, lay horizontal—parallel with the ground. And, like the dead, they don't walk.

In Acts 3, the very next story in the book of Acts after the scenes of Pentecost, Peter and John approach the Beautiful Gate at the temple in Jerusalem. There, at the gate, is the paralyzed Beautiful Gate beggar. It seems from the story that this is how he was known in the community, because that is how people identify him once he starts walking again (Acts 3:10). Peter looks at this man and says to him, "rise!" Some translations of the Bible obscure the original Greek by translating it "get up" or "rise up." Where those translations have two words, the original only has one: "rise!" And it is the same word that Peter has just used on Pentecost for Jesus's resurrection. The man who lays in a posture of death has been told to "rise" by the same prophet of Pentecost who announced the last days. This raised man goes into the temple "walking and leaping and praising God" (Acts 3:8). The wording recalls the end times promises of Isaiah 35:6, which specifically mentions the lame leaping like deer when God restores the fortunes of his people. Jesus's resurrection means not only that these are the last days, but also that healing is already happening.

In Acts 9:32–35, we get another story of a paralyzed man whose name is Aeneas. The story has common elements with the one of the Beautiful Gate beggar, which suggests it is supposed to remind the reader of that story. Aeneas is bedridden, and therefore in a posture of death. Peter says to Aeneas, just as he did to the Beautiful Gate beggar, "rise!" And Aeneas does so "immediately." Again, the word "rise" is the same word routinely used for Jesus's resurrection in the book of Acts. Immediately following Aeneas' mini-resurrection Peter goes to Joppa where he will give the same command, "rise!" to the deceased Tabitha (Acts 9:40). Tabitha's resuscitation is just another instance of a resurrection-command raising people from the posture of death.

· · ·

Right above the doorway of Resurrection Assembly's sanctuary in simple black letters on a taupe-colored wall are the words from John 5:8—"rise, pick up your bed and walk." These are the words Jesus himself said to the paralyzed man at the five-colonnade Sheep Gate pool in Jerusalem. As a church, we want to speak this to every person who walks through our doors. And we do. The meaning of the words unfold with proclamation from the pulpit. By it we mean you must be baptized. By it we mean the lame will leap in the temple today. And by it we mean the dead will rise imperishable tomorrow.

I note the simplicity of the design of the words arching over the doorway because it is itself an image that lives out the scene with Peter, John, and the Beautiful Gate beggar. In my tenure as lead pastor of Resurrection Assembly we have been a poor church. Even so, this allows us to speak the words of Peter with the deepest conviction: "silver and gold we have not, but what we do have we give; in the name of Jesus Christ of Nazareth, rise!" (Acts 3:6).

Altar Calls

The proclamation that Jesus is the soon coming king demands a response. For Peter on the day of Pentecost, some in the crowd "received his word and were baptized" (Acts 2:41). At Resurrection Assembly, we expect the same to happen. This is why, at the end of every sermon, before we approach the communion table, we invite all to confess their sins and—if they haven't been already—to get baptized. This is all following the model set forth on the day of Pentecost.

The proclamation that Jesus heals today also demands a response. And so we expect people to be healed, like the Beautiful Gate beggar and Aeneas were. As we conclude the eucharistic prayer, we invite those who are sick, suffering, or who know someone who is sick or suffering to come to the altar to receive prayer. We make clear that even those who might be refraining from communion are nevertheless heartily invited to receive prayer. We follow the pattern laid out for us in James 5:13–16. It instructs those who are sick to be anointed with oil by the elders of the church: "the prayer of faith will save the one who is sick, the Lord will raise him up" (Jas 5:15).

There are two matters worth noting about James 5 and our liturgy at Resurrection. In addition to inviting people to receive healing of their ailments, James 5:13–16 invites people to be healed of their sins. James says that if anyone has committed sins, they will also be healed of them. James holds together the confession of sin and sickness as both matters that need healing. This is not to suggest that sickness is a direct result of personal sin, but it does mean these matters need to be held together in prayer. This is another reason why we confess our sins before coming to communion, and then as we are serving communion, we invite people not only to receive anointing and prayer for sickness, but also for the sins they have committed.

The second matter is to note that James uses the same language for healing that we encountered in Acts. James says that if someone is anointed with oil and is prayed over by the elders of the church, the Lord will "raise him up." James, like Acts, is using resurrection language to describe what is happening in a healing. This not only connects our prayer for the sick theologically with the proclamation of our soon-returning resurrected Lord in the pulpit, but it also might be the reason James holds the forgiveness of sins and healing together in this passage. Resurrection is the ultimate healing, and we can only attain the ultimate healing of resurrection if our sins are forgiven.

Both responses are part of what we call an "altar call" in Pentecostalism. It is an invitation for people to step out of their seats, walk to the altar of the church as a way of putting their bodies where their mouths and hearts are. This is also why when we serve communion, we invite people to come receive it at the front of the church. That way it is an act of the whole church, and, again, it sets the whole church as the stage of our liturgical performance.

But there is a more typically Pentecostal aspect to our altar call as well. As people come to receive communion, they are welcome to receive prayer and anointing from the elders of the church. But we also always invite people to kneel (or if they are physically unable, to stand) at the altar in prayer to consecrate themselves to God and pray in response to what was preached in the sermon. The altar call is the place where we expect the Holy Spirit to set peoples' hearts on fire with love for God, even as they recognize their Lord in the breaking of bread.

One Sunday morning, about two years or so into my pastorate, we celebrated the Lord's Supper as normal, and invited the sick to receive prayer. Unprompted, a number of people started kneeling at the altar in prayer. No exhortation. No instructions. No words were even spoken. The Holy Spirit simply moved people to kneel in consecration before the risen Lord. Since that Sunday, we have been able to invite people to pray at the altars because it is now clear that, as with everything else in our liturgy, we are simply trying to form our habits. Bending our knees in prayer is a habit worth forming since it is precisely what we will do on the Last Day. Even those who can't kneel now because of physical disabilities will do so, for the resurrection will be their healing: "every knee will bow, and every tongue will confess that Jesus Christ is Lord to the glory of God the Father" (Phil 2:10–11).

We were overjoyed that the Spirit moved in this way because we had faced somewhat of a hurdle in implementing a call to the altar into our liturgy. Specifically, we didn't want to shame or manipulate the congregation into an emotional frenzy. In some Pentecostal circles, it is common practice for the preacher to extend a call to the altar, camp meeting-style, with a long, drawn out, emotionally charged appeal. The intentions are most likely pure: The preacher, we are told, is supposed to do everything possible to persuade the congregation to come to the altar, and by so doing, make a permanent change to their lives by the power and presence of the Holy Spirit.

The problem with this practice is that altar calls have a habit of being more of a threat than an invitation. Preachers will often belabor specific sins, convince the audience they are guilty of said sins, and that if they don't approach the altar then and there, they might just be stuck with the chains of those sins forever. Instead, we wanted to proclaim the Lord who said, "Come to me all who are weary and burdened, and I will give you rest" (Matt 11:28). The problem is that when altar calls are so often associated with this kind of manipulation, it is hard to untangle that sort of abusive spirituality from the act of kneeling at an altar. Coming forward for communion and prayer with the elders of the church was our first step in that direction. When the entire church comes to the altar, it is an act of the whole body, not just for those who have some specific sins they need to address. We were then also faithful in observing communion and James 5. Then, the Holy Spirit did what only he could do. We are grateful that the Spirit did the rest.

Prophetic Confrontation

Physical and psychological illness is incongruous with the new heavens and new earth. That is why we prophesy and say that, at Resurrection Assembly—as in all of God's church—we believe that God will heal today. We pray in faith for healing, believing that the Holy Spirit, who is poured out like oil, is our healing ointment. Just as we can't see the Spirit in the form of a Dove or hear the Father's voice with our ordinary ears at baptism, we may not be able to see our healing, but it is the promise we have in Christ. And promises are as real now as they will be when Christ appears.

But Christ's promise of healing extends beyond the bodies of individuals in the church. We are called to prophetically confront the ailments that afflict the body of Christ as a whole as well. Christ will come tomorrow, so what does that mean for the church today? This is where our end times preaching rubber hits the road. There are innumerable examples to offer, but I will limit myself to two: immigration and debt.

. . .

First, immigration. Resurrection Assembly, as I have said, has people from a number of countries. But that is, in a sense, an inaccurate way of putting it. We are all actually from the same country: the kingdom of God. We are because we will be. That is the promise of our heavenly citizenship.

This is a matter worth proclaiming no matter the political climate. But in view of the ongoing culture wars in the United States over immigration, the southern border, and welcoming refugees, the stakes are much higher. We, the church, must confront all the political rhetoric about immigration with prophecy—prophecy of a coming kingdom where every tongue from every tribe confesses Jesus is Lord as they bend the knee.

I have confronted the matter of immigration from the pulpit by using the analogy of United States embassies around the world. No matter what country you are in, if you step foot onto the property of a US embassy, the United States government considers that US soil. If another country attacks a US embassy, that is considered an attack on US soil. I have said that the same holds true for the church. No matter what country you are in, when you step foot through the doors of the church, you are standing on the same soil you were standing on if you attended another church in another part of the world.

In view of this, I have told immigrants to the United States that they are not immigrants in the church. They required no passport to enter Resurrection Assembly, just as they required no passport to enter their home church in, for example, Bukavu in the Kivu region of the Democratic Republic of Congo. Or, I have put it another way: we are all immigrants at Resurrection Assembly of God, whether we were born inside or outside the United States. Our passport for citizenship was our baptism. Our pledge of allegiance to the crucified God is our weekly celebration of his sacrifice in the Lord's Supper. This means we are not an "American" church that welcomes "immigrants." When Omari Kabwe and his family received American citizenship, we were sure to celebrate with them at church. But I took the opportunity to remind the American-born Christians in the church that Omari and his family were already our fellow citizens in the kingdom, long before they ever stepped foot on US soil.

Calling the church an embassy is profoundly biblical. Moses, the slave-born Israelite in Egypt who had no inheritance in the land, wasn't even an immigrant to the land of Midian because he was nationless. But God met him in the wilderness in the burning bush (Exod 3:1–22), and the ground upon which he stood was called holy. This was not because of anything intrinsic to the land, but because God was present in the fire. That fire was the same fire of the tongues of Pentecost that appeared when people from "every nation under the heavens" (Acts 2:5) were in Jerusalem. It is the same fire of the seven torches—which are the seven spirits of God—in the heavenly throne room in John's apocalypse (Rev 4:5). And it is the same fire that burns in our hearts when Resurrection Assembly gathers on a small plot of land at 1330 Keokuk Street in Iowa City, Iowa.

. . .

Second, debt. I have said almost no one at Resurrection Assembly has much money to speak of. We are a church of the poor, to the poor, and for the poor. We don't have much money, but we do have a lot of debt. This, too, we prophesy against.

The debt industry in the United States is, at best, a new form of indentured servitude, and at worst, the new slavery. Not all forms of slavery are equally brutal, but we nevertheless need to call slavery what it is. Whether it is car debt, credit card debt, school debt, medical debt, house debt, or living-expense debt through agencies like pay-day loan companies, debt controls the lives of the poor (and sometimes the rich) in America. It is indentured servitude because people are lured into debt with promises of eventual freedom. But debt companies are wise enough to know that if they portray themselves as a friend and as a resource in time of need, they can escape the title of "slave-master." Their work is insidiously evil: they claim to do the poor a favor by offering "affordable payments." However, affordable payments are always less than interest accrual, which means the principal is never reduced. And if the principal is never reduced, then payments are—literally—infinite. Freedom never comes. When you work for your profits to go to another, and when you will do this all your life, that—there is no other way to put it!—is slavery.

Nevertheless, where the Spirit of the Lord is, there is freedom. In late 2018, Pastor Abby Anderson took stock of the overwhelming debt the congregants of Resurrection Assembly had and felt led by the Spirit to begin praying for debt cancellation. We invited the church to pray with us, and we prayed for cancelled debts from the pulpit week after week. In a matter of months, we testified to about $42,000 of debt cancelled. There were other unquantifiable debts cancelled as well. People were given free cars, costly lawsuits were dropped, and people were offered new jobs to better meet their living expenses.

While these testimonies were coming in, I prophesied debt forgiveness on Easter 2019. I didn't contrive it, nor did I have a vision from heaven. But our intentional prayers and our engagement with Scriptures led to what the Spirit could only be saying. We are the baptized church whose inheritance is in the life of the world to come. Even the greediest debt collector can't keep us enslaved once we're dead. Because we are baptized, we have died in Christ. Not only that—we are raised in him, and we now walk in newness of life (cf. Rom 6:4). And that newness will carry us into the kingdom. In the sermon, I said, "we're already dead, and that means our debts are already forgiven—the debt collectors just haven't gotten the notice yet." We look forward to the great and unending Jubilee that Christ's return will bring.

Someone in the congregation expressed concern that my words were too radical. Would someone be tempted to default on their debts? And isn't it the right thing to pay the debts for which one signs a promissory note? These are slave owner-type questions. The rich can strategically default on loans for their financial benefit (I personally know someone with riches who did this), yet we are hesitant to hold them to the same standard.

As far as I know, no one at Resurrection Assembly has willingly failed to keep their promises. Nevertheless, we have resolved to join our voice with Moses and with Jesus. They said in word and in deed, "Let my people go!" The delay between the announcement of jubilee and the reality of our freedom in the kingdom is only a delay for the sake of Pharaoh. God wants even the slave owners to repent. And sometimes they do. Zacchaeus, for one, heard Christ's command.

We will leave Egypt tomorrow.

Today, Zacchaeus joins the Jubilee.

Questions for Reflection and Discussion

1. Take stock of several sermons from the last year at your church, paying special attention to how sermons are concluded. What are the common themes and highlights? What immediate action is the church routinely called to?

2. How is your church confronting biblical illiteracy in the American church? How do you model good Bible reading habits at church? Identify one new thing your church can do to increase biblical literacy.

3. What major social problems do people in your church face? How is the church confronting those problems biblically and prophetically?

Slow Burn Revival

When I was first appointed to the lead pastorate in 2016, the church was in a bad place. But the kingdom of God was present. If there is any how-to advice on revitalizing a church that is about to close its doors, it is this: Look for what the Spirit is doing, then fan into flame the gift that is already within the church.

Pentecostals like to talk about revival. The Azusa Street Revival of 1906 continues to play on the imagination of Pentecostals across the world. Revivals are often spoken of in terms of fire. The Bible says that God is an all-consuming fire, after all. Revivals, Pentecostals believe, are when the Spirit of God brings a dead church and a dead society back to life. Thousands, maybe tens or hundreds of thousands, will be saved if the right conditions are set for the Spirit to move. Fire, once hot enough and big enough and wild enough, consumes everything in its path.

Revival is what we wanted in and through our little church in Iowa City. "Revival," which literally means "to live again," is just another word for "resurrection." We believed that God would—and we continue to believe that God will—consume our church, our church neighborhood, and the city of Iowa City with his holy fire and so give new life to those who are still in their sins. The Holy Spirit doesn't destroy. He removes the dross of death because he is the Lord, the Giver of Life.

Well over a year into my pastorate, we put on a poetry slam for the community. It was an outreach of sorts in that we were trying to get new people through the doors of the church, but we have always been against bait-and-switch evangelism techniques where a church lures people in only to try to shove the gospel down their throats when they least expect it. So we invited both Christian and non-Christian poets to perform and one musical artist. And we offered it for free. We wanted to show generosity both to the community at large and to local artists for their talent and contribution to human flourishing. I had high hopes that we'd pack out the sanctuary with new faces. But no one showed up. I mean, some did. But hardly anyone from the church came, and no one from the neighborhood. The people who did come were from a sister church—precisely the people who wouldn't be coming to join us for Sunday worship. This discouraged me. How were we ever going to reach people with the good news of Jesus Christ if we couldn't even get them through the doors with a no-risk, no-strings-attached, free invitation to a community poetry event?

At the event, I expressed my discouragement to one of our lay leaders. He looked at me and said, "slow burn revival." This was prophetic. To be sure, there are times when God sends fire from heaven like he did for Elijah on Mt. Carmel. Not just sacrifices, but barrels and trenches of water and the stones were licked up by the flames of heaven. God's fire, however, doesn't always lick up and consume in a moment. Sometimes, God's fire is the charcoal that stays lit over the long haul. You can pour water on it, you can restrict the oxygen, but it won't be snuffed out through the night. This is the kind of fire that has sustained the church for over two thousand years.

Jesus met his disciples at charcoal fire after his resurrection. He was grilling fish, and had some bread ready to eat. The disciples had been fishing when they heard Jesus tell them from the shore to throw their nets to the other side of their boat. They didn't realize it was him until they came ashore. After seeing him, the charcoal fire, the fish, and the bread, they turned around to count: 153 large fish in their net.

This is a picture of Resurrection Assembly of God in Iowa City. We are the charcoal fire where Jesus stands ready to feed the world. When the fire comes from heaven, we don't want to be consumed like straw. We want to catch it, and burn in the presence of Jesus for hours, days, years—we want to burn with a steady, quiet, and unquenchable fire until the Last Day. Our Pentecostal liturgy is how we do that.

Fanning Into Flame

As I have said, the kingdom of God was present despite the church being in a bad place. The fire had not gone out from the leftover coals. And Jesus was feeding people bread and grilled fish through the faithful hands of Pastor Abby Anderson and her husband Kyle. More specifically, these people were the kids and teens. Seeing that Jesus was with them and that he had sent his fiery Spirit in their midst, the first step in revitalizing the church—the first step toward revival—was to fan into flame the gift that was already there.

The Pentecostal liturgy described in this book was in a sense constructed for the kids. We thought to ourselves, "How do we disciple the kids?" And then we did what we discerned through the Spirit we ought to do. We of course drew on much of the historic church's liturgies through the Apostles' and Nicene Creeds, and through the eucharistic prayer we prayed. But, in the first instance, we wanted to disciple the kids biblically. What we did was what has been described in this book. We baptized the unbaptized kids. We taught them to pray the Lord's Prayer. We invited them to the Lord's Table. We proclaimed to them that they live God's story that begins with creation and will culminate in the resurrection of the dead and the life of the world to come.

The kids were fanned into flame. They were not only discipled, they began leading in church. They led the church in prayer, including the Lord's Prayer. They became the offering ushers. They led the recitation of the creeds. They served communion. They led songs of praise from the altar. And the fire of the Lord of Life, through them, spread to the whole church.

Liturgy for Everyone

Resurrection Assembly, as I have said, is an incredibly diverse group of people. People from every walk of life have come through the church. The homeless, the disabled, rural white Iowans, the educated so-called "elite," immigrants and refugees, black Chicagoans and Latinos, and the urban poor all worship the risen Lord side-by-side. I have had people outside of the church—even non-Christians—ask me how it is possible that such a diverse group of people can all be gathered together. In these moments, it is tempting to appeal to my own credentials. I grew up in West Africa and therefore speak French (there is a disproportionate number of French-speaking Africans in Johnson County, Iowa). I also attended two of the Western world's elite educational institutions for my master's and doctoral degrees. But those factors only have limited explanatory power. And face to face with God, my credentials are rubbish anyway.

At the end of the day there is only one thing to say: That which brings together such a diverse and disparate group is the risen Lord, Jesus Christ. He has poured out his Holy Spirit upon us, and the Spirit is our unity in human diversity. We give him thanks for the miracle that Resurrection Assembly is.

But God also requires faithfulness from us. And we can quench the Spirit such that unity is broken and barricades to re-unification are erected. The extent to which we have been faithful in fostering place where the Spirit's unity is celebrated and embraced is the extent to which we have shown hospitality to kids. This is the concluding claim of this book: If you welcome kids, you welcome everyone. If you disciple kids, you disciple everyone. Liturgies for kids are liturgies for everyone.

This may seem like too rigid a claim, but it becomes obvious when you think about it. Children have no money, so if you welcome them into your liturgy, you welcome the poor. Children come to church needing their entire understanding of the Christian faith to be built from the ground up. If you build them up, you build up everyone. If you are careful to unpack the heaviest and most complicated concepts of the faith to kids, you show the same hospitality to people whose first language is not English. And you do the same for the intellectually disabled. If you inspire children with the mystery of the gospel, you can inspire even the most imagination-less adult. If you are sensitive to the ways in which children are treated in the West as second-class citizens, you can be sensitive to the ways in which many adults—whether they be a single mother, a black American, or an immigrant—are discriminated against in subtle but profound ways. If you believe that kids can be baptized in the Holy Spirit and speak in other tongues, you believe anyone can receive the Holy Spirit.

Jesus not only said, "let the little children come to me" (Matt 19:14). He also said, "unless you turn and become like children, you will never enter the kingdom of heaven" (Matt 18:3). The task of liturgy is therefore not only to show hospitality to children, but to invite everyone to become children.

Liturgy as Discipleship

I draw this book to a close by stating something that has been implied throughout this book, but needs to be said explicitly: Liturgy is discipleship. Christian disciples worship and proclaim the risen Lord. So we ought to have patterns of worship that train people to do that very thing. Discipleship is not something that happens outside of regular Christian worship. Worship ought to be the place where we learn and perform faith that we live. I have spoken of the sabbathless society we live in. I have also spoken of the plummeting rates of biblical literacy in the West. How we worship ought to be remedying these ailments of the church.

This book could be rewritten as a catechism—a paradigm of discipleship for new Christians. And in fact, we do follow its patterns when we disciple people in preparation for baptism. We teach people who seek baptism to pray the Lord's Prayer, to recite the creeds, and we teach them Christian love through the Ten Commandments. But we would be squandering that preparation if baptized Christians see no obvious connection between what they learn in discipleship and experience in baptism, and what the church does in worship. The liturgy described in this book is thus both a confirmation of and a performance of the discipleship Christians receive leading up to their baptisms.

Every week, we come back to the basics at Resurrection Assembly. We remember our baptisms. We remember the covenant of Jesus's body and blood. And we look forward to Christ's soon return. This liturgy is the steady flow of oxygen on our slow burn revival.

Questions for Reflection and Discussion

1. How healthy is your church? Is it vibrant with life, sickly, or near death? What past habits and practices is God freeing your church from that will make way for new life?

2. Revisit Q1 from the Introduction: Where is the kingdom of God present, and how can you fan it into flame?

3. Are children involved and welcomed at every level of your church's worship? Why or why not?

4. If the Sunday service is the only time some people come to church, how are they being discipled by the liturgy?

Epilogue

Prophetic Motherhood

In 2023, a transition took place at the church. I stepped down from the lead pastorate, and Abby Anderson took charge. I remain at the church part-time with the title "pastor of preaching and theology." My full-time job at the time of composition is as director of theology at the College of Online Learning at Evangel University. Since it is an online program, I'm able to stay in Iowa City and continue to minister at the church.

Nearly from the beginning, Abby and I formed a partnership and co-led the revitalization of the church. So the transition to her leadership was a fitting and predictable one. Throughout the years, it became clear to me that God had placed me at Resurrection for the particular purpose of facilitating her rise to leadership. As I got to know her, it quickly became clear to me not only that God had called her to lead a church sometime, but that the church she would lead would be the one I was then in charge of.

I don't remember when, but I started calling Abby the "mother of the church." The title seemed fitting because she always had children in her wake, though none of them were biologically her own because she was medically unable to bear children. Not only the kids, but she was also there when no other pastoral leadership was. For the year or so that the church was without a lead pastor, she remained. Other pastors and leadership in the Assemblies of God counseled her and Kyle, her husband, to leave, but they refused. She nurtured what was there, and it was her caring, gentle, maternal, Spirit-led patience that would ultimately give birth to the revival we saw and continue to see at the church.

As I have detailed in the book, the church—like Abby—appeared by all worldly standards to be infertile. But God worked a miracle, and Resurrection has baptized many sons and daughters for the kingdom. Similarly, after years of my prayers and others', Abby conceived a child and gave birth. Zion Anderson is one small testimony that no womb, and therefore no church, is ever outside of God's reach to make into a hospitable, nurturing, life-giving source for his kingdom.

Life bursts forth from elderly, infertile, and virginal wombs in the Bible. And it emerges from tombs. As I've said over and over in this book, the Life himself (as the Gospel of John calls our Lord) emerged from the grave. There, in the garden, Mary stood weeping in front of the tomb. Jesus asked her, "woman, why are you weeping?" She wanted Jesus's body back. She soon realizes it's her Lord, and then rushes to announce the resurrection of the dead in and through Jesus to the apostles (John 20:15). Abby is in Mary's kingdom lineage. Her love for Christ's body has been evident through tears, disappointment, confusion, heaviness, and the apparent final word of death. It's now also evident in her Spirit-filled joy every Resurrection Sunday morning when we meet Jesus in our garden-like sanctuary.

The church is in decline in the United States. I've detailed our Pentecostal liturgy, and the ways in which we recognized what the Holy Spirit was already doing so we could fan a revival into flame. But I'm compelled also to say that if we want to see God revive his church, we must recognize those whom he has anointed with the Holy Spirit to preach good news. Daughters prophesy. Mary the Virgin sang a song that reverberates through the ages. Mary Magdalene was the first to proclaim that Christ is risen.

Abby continues that feminine tradition.

Bibliography

Budde, Michael. *The Borders of Baptism: Identities, Allegiances, and the Church.* Eugene, OR: Cascade, 2011.

Earls, Aaron. "Protestant Church Closures." https://research.lifeway.com/2021/05/25/protestant-church-closures-outpace-openings-in-u-s/.

———. "Small Churches." https://research.lifeway.com/2021/10/20/small-churches-continue-growing-but-in-number-not-size/.

Simatupang, Florian. *The Eucharist Spirit: A Renewal Theology of the Lord's Supper.* Eugene, OR: Wipf & Stock, forthcoming.

Hollenweger, Walter. *The Pentecostals: The Charismatic Movement in the Churches.* Peabody, MA: Hendrickson, 1988.

Jenson, Robert. *Systematic Theology: The Works of God.* Oxford: Oxford University Press, 1999.

Pelikan, Jaroslav. *The Vindication of Tradition.* New Haven: Yale University Press, 1984.

Read more of Joseph Lear's writing here:

www.ingramcontent.com/pod-product-compliance
Lightning Source LLC
Chambersburg PA
CBHW020212090426
42734CB00008B/1029